DEDICATION

The sport of harness racing is colorful and exciting and its popularity has endured through many challenges. Yet for the horsemen and horsewomen who make the sport happen, it's an occupation that requires unbelievably hard work and dedication. They train their horses in the morning and race them in the afternoon and evening. They work on holidays. If they're lucky, they take a Sunday off here or there. And they do all this having no idea what their income might be, as no one can predict what horses will earn.

Yet through it all, our horsemen and horsewomen — some with legacies in the business reaching back as far as five generations — have propelled Pennsylvania harness racing to a premier position in the industry. In doing so, they've created jobs for many thousands of Pennsylvania residents — as well as valuable tax revenue for the state —while providing entertainment for millions of fans throughout the Commonwealth.

The Keystone Chapter of the United States Harness Writers Association conceived this volume as a way of commemorating and publicizing the commitment, talent and vision of Pennsylvania's horsemen and horsewomen. This book is dedicated to them.

CONTENTS

BOOK ONE
"The Origin of Harness Racing"

HARNESS RACING IN THE KEYSTONE STATE

VICTORIA HOWARD

AuthorHouse™
1663 Liberty Drive
Bloomington, IN 47403
www.authorhouse.com
Phone: 833-262-8899

This book is printed on acid-free paper.

*Permission was granted for all photos.

*Front cover designed by Chris Gooden.

ISBN: 978-1-6655-7362-7 (sc)
ISBN: 978-1-6655-7364-1 (hc)
ISBN: 978-1-6655-7363-4 (e)

Print information available on the last page.

Published by AuthorHouse 11/08/2022

authorHOUSE®

PHOTO GALLERY

BOOK TWO

"It Takes A Village"

ACKNOWLEDGEMENTS

Writing the history of harness racing was exciting and educational but also challenging, for obtaining actual facts from the 1800s was harder than I imagined.

Although I am basically the author, there are many people who assisted with the final production of this book for, *"It takes a village to achieve anything great."*

I want to thank Bob Marks, Jerry Connors, Jake Hoover, Rick Kane, Heather Wilder, Roger Huston, Jeff Zidek, Curby Stillings, Chris Gooden, Jennifer Starr, Dawnelle Mock, and historian Nancy McAfoose, who submitted factual information on the Indiana County Fair that began in 1852.

A very special thanks goes to Evan Pattak who took on the extremely difficult task of editing the entire book, making sure the contents was accurate. I could not have done this without you! My deepest appreciation!

Though there may be some people not mentioned in the book, we tried to include a little about all horsemen who provided information about their relatives. Some may not be with us today, but nonetheless, they are just as important to the sport as the people still with us.

"Opening Night at The Meadows"
June 28, 1963

"Opening Night at Pocono Downs"
1966

“Delvin Miller”

PREFACE

HARNESS RACING IN THE KEYSTONE STATE is a combination history, reference, and coffee-table book, comprised of a photo gallery and racing tidbits. Within the binding are two books.

Book One is the history of racing horses, starting with chariot racing in 753 BC to the present day of harness racing, and an overview of harness racing's greatest progenitors: *Messenger, Abdullah* and *Hambletonian*.

Also covered are the origin of Pennsylvania Fair Racing commencing in the 1800s through the present day and highlights of Pennsylvania's premier racetracks: *Liberty Bell Park, Hollywood Casino at the Meadows, The Downs at Mohegan Sun Pocono,* and *Harrah's Philadelphia Casino & Racetrack*.

Enclosed in the middle of the two books is a photo gallery adorned with over 100 priceless images -- some taken as early as the 1800s.

Book Two is more contemporary, showcasing management, trainers, drivers, "people behind the scenes," game changers, prominent owners and generations of harness racing families.

I hope this book rekindles wonderful memories for those enamored with our sport and its two-and four-legged legends, and that this history will be passed down from generation to generation.

BOOK ONE

"The Origin of Harness Racing"

CHAPTER ONE

In The Beginning

"Chariot Racing: The Origin of Harness Racing"

EVOLUTION OF THE HORSE

Let's begin with the star of harness racing: the horse.

The evolution of the horse occurred over a geologic period of 50 million years, transforming the animal from the small, dog-sized Eohippus into today's modern horse.

Much of the evolution took place in North America where horses originated but became extinct about 10,000 years ago.

The horse belongs to the order Perissodactyla (meaning odd-toed ungulates), the members of which all share 'hooved' feet and an odd number of toes on each foot, as well as the upper and a similar tooth structure.

Its features were flexible legs, four toes on each front foot, and three on the hind feet.

The early ancestors of the modern horse walked on several spread-out toes, an accommodation to life spent walking on the soft, moist ground of forests.

Wild horses have been known since prehistoric days from central Asia to Europe. When the Spanish colonists brought domestic horses from Europe, many escaped.

The sport of what would become known as "harness racing" originated in the eighth century BC with chariot racing when Romulus constructed the very first known racetrack, the Circus Maximus. The contests held went on to be the most popular sporting events in Ancient Rome.

Chariot races weren't quite as gruesome as the death matches between gladiators that Romans staged for audiences; thus, this form of entertainment would evolve into the sport of harness racing centuries later.

BLAME IT ON HOLLYWOOD

Perhaps you can "Blame it on Hollywood," for movies illustrated what could be the start of our sport. The initial chariot racing seen in the movies was when the immortal Ben Hur (assuming he was actually a real person) drove a horse pulling a chariot around the Coliseum.

Other countries followed suit, especially the Greeks and the Egyptians, as horse-drawn chariots were not only utilized for racing purposes, but they also served as army vehicles carrying archers and soldiers in the ongoing Mediterranean wars between the various nations.

It was horse-drawn chariots that Egyptian Pharaoh Ramses utilized to pursue Moses and the Israelites that were swallowed up by the parting of the Red Sea, according to legend.

For thousands of years, horse-pulled chariots, carriages and wagons were utilized to transport people and supplies from one place to another.

The history of modern-day harness racing begins with the commencement of the horse breed that came to be known as the Standardbred. The competitive racing of horses is one of man's most ancient sports and was inaugurated with the Assyrian kings of 1500 BC; they kept elaborate stables, and the trainers drove chariots.

Chariot racing was one of the most famous sports in the ancient Byzantine, Roman, Iranian and Greek periods.

In Rome, public records were kept of the bloodlines of horses, and exceptional horses were buried with their records. The average race began with a *pompa* (procession), beginning at the Capitoline Hill through the Forum and Sacred Way, and back towards Forum Boarium.

Horses were worthy of reputation and respect for their prowess in races, and the drivers were equally as popular. The most famous charioteer, Polydus' horse, *Compressor,* was even depicted in mosaics.

Caligula, the third of Rome's emperors (formerly known as Gaius), had a favorite horse named *Incitatus,* a white stallion and former racehorse.

If Caligula loved anything, it was this handsome steed. In fact, the horse had 18 servants, was fed oats mixed with gold flakes, and his stable was made of the best marble. *Incitatus* was treated and lived better than most of the townspeople.

Since the color purple has always represented royalty, only purple blankets of the finest material were worn by *Incitatus,* and a halter of precious stones adorned the steed's head.

Wanting to continue the *Incitatus* line, Caligula gave his beloved stallion a wife--a mare named Penelope. It is also said that Caligula claimed his horse to be a "combination of all the gods" and to be worshipped as one.

Chariot drivers became celebrities who had "groupies" that followed their every race. The champion, 27-year-old Flavius Scorpus, was a slave, as were many of the charioteers. The young Roman rode for the Green faction and won over 2048 races out of 4,257 before being killed in a racetrack collision.

Ironically, mares were seldom used as lead horses but occasionally occupied inside positions.

Chariot racing continued in the Byzantine Era (Eastern Roman Empire) where cheating, gambling and bribes were common.

In the neighboring country of Greece, chariot racing was also one of the most popular sports and played an essential role in aristocratic funeral games.

In Egypt, chariots were known as the "racing cars of the ancient world," first appearing about 1600 BC. Quickly they became not only the preferred mode of transportation for royalty and the elite, but they also revolutionized military tactics and warfare.

In 1978, remains of chariots were discovered in Egyptian tombs. Tutankhamun's (King Tut) tomb contained six chariots, which tripled the number of Egyptian chariots known before the discovery of the tomb.

The discovery was not in perfect condition and required very careful examination. The chariots' remains were covered in coral, which made them difficult to see, but it appears the coral was used at the time to help preserve them.

Chariots and horses have also played a huge role in history for racing, war, and hunting. Unfortunately, the exciting Ben Hur sport of chariot racing virtually disappeared with the fall of the Roman Empire. In many ways the sport of chariot racing paved the way for harness racing, which would be introduced centuries thereafter.

The history of modern-day harness racing begins with the commencement of the horse breed that came to be known as the Standardbred.

Pennsylvania's earliest organized harness races took place during the 1800s at county fairs where families would bring their "best" horses to compete against one another.

In addition, many farmers would ship their carriage horses to the county fairs to compete in what were called at that time "speed trials." Consequently, harness racing was often referred to as the "farmer's sport."

MESSENGER
1780-1808

"The Founding Sire of the Standardbred"

In 1780, English colonists imported *Mes*senger, an 8-year-old grey

Thoroughbred (sired by *Mambrino* out of an unnamed turf mare by *Turf) t*o the United States, hoping to replenish the horse racing stock that had perished when the Revolutionary War broke out.

After days sailing in a cramped confinement, *Messenger* charged down the plank while disembarking so boisterously that it took two men to contain him. The stallion showed more strength than beauty and was tough to handle.

Messenger was inbred to *Cade* in the third and fourth generations. Although his sire was a trotter, *Messenger* never competed in a trot race. While still in England, *Messenger* started in 16 flat races, winning 10 of them.

Not particularly handsome, *Messenger* had large, active ears, a bony head, a Roman nose, huge nostrils and stood 15.3 hands high.

When arriving in America, *Messenger* was bred throughout Pennsylvania, New York and New Jersey. He sired not only great Thoroughbreds but is also considered "The Founding Father of the Harness Horse."

Messenger was extremely fertile and is said to have bred 126 mares by natural cover one season. The bloodline of *Messenger* shows up in countless Thoroughbred champions such as, *Man O' War, Whirlaway, Seabiscuit, Gallant Fox* and others.

ABDULLAH
1823-1854

"A Grandson of Messenger"

In 1805, at the age of 25, *Messenge*r sired the bay colt *Mambrino* --- named after his own sire. In that era before a formal registry was established, a repetition of names was common.

Mambrino showed an impeccable trotting gait and thus was listed as a natural trotter who was 'clear, square and distinct.'

Son *Mambrino's* "claim to fame" won his only race, but *Mambrino's* real masterpiece came through his own son, *Abdullah,* out of *Amazonia* --- a renowned trotting mare able to trot a mile under saddle faster than 3:00, a time then that was considered incomprehensible.

Abdullah, a dark colt, rather leggy with a slim body, was foaled in 1823. He was probably the most remarkable trotting sire ever produced on this continent. Because the stallion was said to lack brain balance and was extremely nervous, *Abdullah* was rejected by the Breeders of Orange County and removed from that county.

Of his physical attraction it was said that he had extremely long, very thin and sharp ears, thus any horse like this was marked as being an *"Abdullah – ear."*

As was the custom with stallions at that time, *Abdullah,* who had never trained or raced, began serving mares at age 3. At age 4, *Abdullah* was lightly trained and trotted an exhibition mile in 3:10 under saddle.

In 1854, *Abdullah* was sent to a farmer who promised to give the horse a forever home, but later that year the farmer reneged on the deal and sold *Abdullah* for a mere $35 to a fishmonger. Upon returning home, the new owner hooked *Abdullah* to a wagon. Even at the ripe age of 31, *Abdullah* wanted nothing to do with it, kicked the wagon, shattering it to pieces, and broke free. Sadly, *Abdullah* was discovered dead shortly after on Long Island due to neglect and starvation.

Although Abdulla's fate may have been disheartening and unwarranted, only an outline has been given of *Abdullah's* stud career. It might be amplified by many interesting details, but one thing is certain: *Abdullah* was the most successful trotting sire of his generation, siring more race winners than any rival of that day.

His offspring were said to have remarkable gameness and ability to campaign over long stretches of time and go long distances to a sulky, wagon or under saddle.

HAMBLETONIAN
1849-1876

"The Granddaddy of 'Em All"

Hambletonian, an American trotting horse and one of the best trotting horses of the late 18th century, was bred by John Hutchinson and foaled in 1849. He was the American Standardbred racehorse that was the ancestor of most present-day harness racers.

Born in Sugar Loaf, New York, *Hambletonian* was a muscular bay colt with a white star on his head, white hind ankles, perfect conformation, and would become the thrice-inbred great-grandson of *Messenger* --- and the foundation sire of trotting horses.

Hambletonian's full name was *Hambletonian 10,* but he was also called *Rysdyk's Hambletonian*. Legend has it that his dam was a common, crippled mare named, *Charles Kent,* who before meeting with misfortune, could trot a mile close to 2:40.

When *Charles Kent* proved too lame for roadwork, she was sold to Jonas Seeley, with foal by her side, for $125 to William Rysdyk, a farmhand employed by Seeley. Eventually, Rysdyk became extremely wealthy from *Hambletonian's* stud fees.

Seeley raised two fillies from *Charles Kent* and in 1848 mated her to the great *Abdullah*. The following spring, *Charles Kent* foaled a colt that someday would be one of the greatest sires in history.

Although *Hambletonian* was raced very little, he was placed in stud in 1851. When *Hambletonian* was 3, he was time trialed in 2:48.1. Thereafter, demand for *Hambletonian's* stud services increased, and the original stud fee of $25 skyrocketed to $500.

During his lifetime, *Hambletonian* earned more than $185,700 --- equivalent to several million in today's dollars. Before he died in 1876, *Hambletonian* sired more than 1,000 foals, which dominated the breed noted for their trotting ability.

Harness racing's most prestigious race, The Hambletonian, is named after the great sire *Hambletonian*, and his legacy continues as every Standardbred today traces back to him.

THE ORIGIN OF HARNESS RACING IN AMERICA

By the early 19th century there were many trotting tracks across the United States. In 1806 a horse called *Yankee* trotted a mile over the track in Harlem, New York, with the time of 2:59.

In 1810, the standard was lowered to 2:48.1 by an unnamed trotting gelding from Boston at the Hunting Park track in Philadelphia.

By 1840, trotting competition was an organized sport in New England, and a new era was underway. In 1879, the Standardbred horse was established in the United States, based on a standard of time performance of 2:30 for one mile.

With the popularity of harness racing came the development of the Standardbred --- a horse bred specifically for racing under harness.

INTRODUCING THE STANDARDBRED BREED OF THE TWENTIETH CENTURY

Prior to the commencement of pari-mutuel racing at Liberty Bell Park in northern Philadelphia, the State of Pennsylvania was well entrenched in the production of championship Standardbreds at Hanover Shoe Farms located in southern Pennsylvania near the Maryland border.

Hanover Shoe Farms was established when Harper D. Sheppard and Clinton D. Myers took over a struggling shoe business in 1899 and re-named it Hanover Shoe.

In 1901, Myers and Sheppard opened their first retail store in downtown New York. They managed the shoe manufacturing operation during the week then traveled to New York on Saturday to help with the sales at their retail store for the rest of the day.

The men discovered the most expedient way to cover the long distance between Hanover and New York was with horses, so they began purchasing and developing a stable of fast horses.

Harper's son Lawrence joined his father and Myers in the shoe business until he completed his education and then became active with the horses.

One day when Harper and Myers were away on business Lawrence sold all the horses in the stable and then convinced his father and Myers to invest in better quality stock.

In 1926, Lawrence purchased the entire breeding stock of the estate of noted breeder A. B. Coxe for $150,000. The outstanding collection of stallions and broodmares started Hanover Shoe Farms on the road to becoming a top-class establishment. Nearly three-quarters of a century later, Hanover Shoe Farms continues as the leading money-earning breeder in the sport and has led the annual money-earning totals every year.

Hanover Shoe Farms was initially a world-class producer of trotters, via stallions *Dean Hanover, Nibble Hanover* and *Titan Hanover.* Hanover then became an elite producer of pacers, initially via the location of the ill-fated *Billy Direct,* his optimum son *Tar Heel,* and their association with Delvin Miller's Meadow Lands Farm and *Adios.*

Meanwhile, Del Miller eventually acclaimed as "The World-Class Ambassador Of Harness Racing," started his own breeding establishment in western Pennsylvania, featuring his newly purchased *Adios,* who would eventually be considered among the great progenitors of all time.

It might also be noted that *Meadow Skipper,* another super sire, was foaled and raised at Miller's Meadow Lands Farm. Delvin Miller's farm had a huge impact, putting champion horses and their progeny on the map. Its legacy was and always will be in harness racing.

Hall of Famer Lawrence B. Sheppard's vision of making Hanover Shoe Farms the greatest racing and breeding operation of Standardbreds was quite successful.

By breeding the "best to the best," their present day stallion lineup includes *Captaintreacherous, Greenshoe, Stay Hungry* and *Tall Dark Stranger.* Hanover has been the sport's leading money-winning breeder in each of the last 74 years --- ever since records were first kept in 1949. An unbelievable feat!

THE ORIGIN OF HARNESS RACETRACKS

In the 18th century, roads were restricted to the streets of towns; thus the development of the horse for travel and the growth of harness racing in the streets came to be. Trotters were perfectly happy on the road, and matches between horses were acceptable.

As the sport evolved around cities in the later 18th century, a particular avenue was deemed "best for the racing of horses," which is why Philadelphia and many other cities have to this day a "Race Street" on their maps.

The first known trotting race on a road took place in 1817, 2 miles under saddle on the Jamaica Turnpike, Long Island (for a prize of $1,000). On May 27, 1823, the first track trot was held on the Union Course.

The ensuing years in America brought famous names such as *Paul Pry,* a gelding who won a match race against time: 17 3/4 miles in 58:52 for driver Hiram Woodruff in November 1833.

In 1906, a Connecticut-bred horse named *Yankee* trotted a mile on the road in 2:59. Harness racing became very popular and has grown steadily from the humblest of beginnings into a multi-million dollar business.

The first harness tracks were opened in the mid-800s, although harness racing could be found as early as the 1800s at county fairs.

EARLY HORSE RACING IN PENNSYLVANIA

Though late to the game of legalized horse racing, Pennsylvania has early ties to both Thoroughbred and harness racing.

Nicknamed "the farmer's sport," harness racing began on the back roads and village streets using wooden buggies as carts. The sport thrived until horse racing came to an abrupt halt when it was banned in 1820 and gambling was forbidden.

To evade the law, people raced trotting horses, mainly used for work and transportation (not just for racing), and therefore were exempt from the ban.

Trotting races drew huge crowds, and the first track dedicated to driving races opened in Philadelphia in the mid 1820s. The races attracted large crowds resulting in a demand for faster and better horses, which paved the way for the establishment and success of Hanover Shoe Farms.

Managed by founder Harper Sheppard's son Lawrence, the farm's goal was to improve the breed and make Hanover the "greatest name in harness racing."

By continuously acquiring well-bred and champion trotting and pacing stallions and mares, Hanover continues today to breed and sell racehorse prospects that have gone on to win classic races, including *The Hambletonian*, *The Little Brown Jug, The Adios* and *The Breeders Crown* series.

By the mid-20th century, harness racing was the fastest growing sport in America. Prior to the establishment of Liberty Bell Park in 1963, many Philadelphians were initially exposed to Delaware's Brandywine Raceway, located just off the south Philadelphia and Pennsylvania border in nearby Delaware.

Although Brandywine was not officially a track located in Pennsylvania, it evolved into a circuit with Liberty Bell, as the two tracks initially did not compete with each other, thus allowing horsemen and Philadelphia fans additional racing dates. Brandywine Raceway was the first track to open in the surrounding area and easily accessible for horsemen and patrons.

Presently, the state of Pennsylvania provides three harness tracks: *The Downs at Mohegan Sun Pocono, Harrah's ® Philadelphia Racetrack & Casino,* and *Hollywood Casino at the Meadows,* as well as fair tracks.

The industry in Pennsylvania is so ingrained with agriculture that even if handle and attendance are somewhat less than what they used to be, the production of Pennsylvania-sired-and-bred trotters and pacers is vital to the economy of the Keystone State.

And anyone who has ever been involved one way or another in the sport will tell you it is an addictive drug; once in your blood, it will always be there.

The sights, sounds and smells of a racetrack -- even the colorful equine and human characters --- are what make us "harness racing addicts."

"Greyhound"

Photo: Courtesy of the Hambletonian Society

"Messenger: The Founding Father of the American Standardbred Horse""

"Hambletonian"

CHAPTER TWO

Pennsylvania County Fairs

"Unidentified Boy Jogging a Horse"

"101 years old, Charles Taylor --- The Oldest Known Man Jogging a Horse in 1907"

The Pennsylvania County Fairs

The history of fairs is clouded as to exactly when the first fair "officially" opened. It is said that fairs and exhibitions came out of 18th century western Europe and were delivered to the colonial docks of Boston and Halifax with a predisposed mission to help serve agriculture and animal husbandry.

This observation ignores the centuries of historical linkage to the eastern Mediterranean before the birth of Christ. Old and New Testament references to fairs are mixed with allusions to commerce, trade, the marketplace, festivals, religious feasts and holy days.

In 1765, less than 300 years after Columbus finished his work in "the New World," the first North American fair was presented in Windsor, Nova Scotia. That same fair continues to operate today.

In the "not-yet-formed" United States, a fair was chartered in York, PA in 1765. County fairs in Pennsylvania are normally held between June and September, although there are a few held in the spring as well as October.

Fairs provide great culture, rides, food, exhibitions, contests --- and harness racing. More recently, some fairs have added to the list of amenities an annual fair beauty pageant for young women.

But a word of advice --- before attending a fair there is one rule: ***throw healthy eating out the window!***

Today, there are approximately 2,000 fairs held in North America each year.

YORK COUNTY FAIR
1765-2022

"America's First Fair"

Beginning in 1765 (10 years before the Declaration of Independence was signed), the York County Fair opened, attracting people from Pennsylvania to Maryland. The racing of Standardbreds featured at the York Fair was popular from the very beginning.

A charter to hold the fair was granted to the people of York by Thomas Penn (son of William Penn) in recognition of "the flourishing state to which the town arrived through their industry."

At that time the York Fair existed as a two-day agricultural market on the town commons, now known as Penn Park.

In 1867, during the harness races it began to downpour so violently that they had to postpone the card. Several days later they ran off the cancelled races in a satisfactory manner until the last race when driver Emanuel King was thrown from his sulky after accidentally running into a skeleton wagon. Luckily, King was unharmed.

The first race offered a $20 purse and had two entries vying for the money. The chestnut sorrel, *Claude,* won in the time of 3:13.

In 1918, the York Fair did not open due to an influenza outbreak that killed 166 people in York. Today, the York County Fair is attended by thousands of people for the demolition derbies, tasty food, thrilling rides and harness racing at its best.

WASHINGTON COUNTY FAIR
1798-2022

"Local Horsemen Set Track Records"

Although the fairs held at Washington County go back to the days when it was a frontier town, the fairgrounds were not purchased until the 1910s.

In the years since, the fairgrounds have expanded with new structures, barns, a huge grandstand and a half-mile track called the Arden Downs Racetrack.

For many years the Washington County Fairgrounds was an important stop on the Grand Circuit of harness racing. In fact, many stakes are named after Arden Downs at The Meadows.

In 2013, the fillies showed up, leaving their mark as they won 11 of the 14 races. Walter "Boots" Dunn's misses swept the 2-year-old filly trot events.

In 2016, Rick Beinhauer set a track record of 2:04.1 with his *Lucky Chucky* filly named *Lovebeinglucky.*

And Aug. 16, 2016, is a day 19-year-old horseman Jeremy Indof will never forget. It was a "once-in-a-lifetime type of experience" for Jeremy as he guided his horse, *I'm Sooo Slick,* to victory in the 2-year-old filly pace -- his first purse race drive.

But probably the most significant fact about the Washington County Fairgrounds is that Hall of Famer Harry Harvey --- a protege of Delvin Miller --- developed the great Albatross there.

Today, the Washington County Fair hosts events that run for two weeks.

Held every August, there are no shortage of 4-H animals, tractor pulls, top entertainment and rides.

"Unidentified Man Warming Up at Washington County Fairgrounds"

ERIE COUNTY FAIR
1820-2022

"America's Fair"

Located on Routes 8 & 89 in Wattsburg, PA, the Erie County Fair provides top entertainers, amusement rides, truck, tractor and horse pulls, and much more.

The Erie County Fair is second home to generations of horsemen; one being the Daugherty family. Says Bill Dougherty, Jr.:

"Back in the 1960s the races were held at night and at that time, there was still a hub rail. They raced two divisions, and the races went in about 2:08 to 2:10 ----a far cry from today.

"It was always very, very foggy, making it difficult to see well. I will always remember the night I was driving one of my father's horses and a line broke in the stretch. Hanging on for dear life and steering the best I could while saying a prayer, I made four laps around the track and still finished second."

In 2019, *Penance*, a 2-year-old Father Patrick gelding, won his fifth "A" fair event in 2:06.3— just three ticks shy of the divisional track record set by *Tag The Lady* 10 years earlier.

DAYTON FAIR
1831-2022

"Tonianne sets two track records"

The Dayton Fair, located in Dayton, Armstrong County, houses a Fair Museum exhibiting just about anything you can think of --- from wooden equipment of the '30s and '40s, an old corn shredder, to a Haflinger treadmill.

Local horseman Bill Daugherty, Jr. remembers the time he won four races in one week with his mare *Gala Gal* at Dayton:

"Gala Gal won two times in the beginning of the week and come back to win two times at the end of the week. It was a great fair to race at for the people were so nice. Gus Burkett was the starter for the races, and he would actually remind the drivers what position they were to get in while they were going to the gate."

Today the week-long fair provides many attractions, exhibits, rides, food, music, camel rides, a game show, a circus, a demolition derby, mud slings, concerts and harness racing. There is something to do for the entire family.

In 2021, the race card did not disappoint when the track record was tied by 3-year-old pacing filly *Tonianne* in 1:58.4 --- equaling *More More More'* s standard set in 2019.

That win earned T*onianne*, a *Somebeachsomewhere* filly, bragging rights as the first horse on the 2021 PA fair circuit to achieve two distinctions: two track records and two miles in 2:00 or less.

Tonianne was driven and trained by Todd Schadel, who also won the three-year-old "A" Sire Stakes trot that day.

BUTLER COUNTY FAIR
1836-2022

"Named after General Butler"

Butler County, founded in 1800, was named for General Richard Butler—an officer in the American Revolution.

In 1836, the Butler County Agricultural Society held its first gathering around the courthouse square. In 1851, the fair was reorganized by the Agricultural Society and relocated to Bigham Grove, a small oak grove north of the city, where it continued until it moved to its present location. At first a small number of horses were displayed, but as the years went by the number of horses increased.

In 1874, a racetrack oval was constructed that was 714 long and 380 feet wide or approximately a half-mile. In a 1-mile race the horses would go around five turns (or need a chute).

During the 1880s and 1890s, the Butler County Fair continued to grow and prosper. In 1913, a fire destroyed the old wooden grandstand, but it was replaced that year with a 3,000-seat facility that cost $33,000.

Since then additional improvements have been made, such as the construction of several barns and a larger hall for floral and produce exhibits.

Today, the Butler Fair boasts a collection of attractions like the Ferris Wheel, The Claw, The Ring of Fire and many other thrilling rides.

CRAWFORD COUNTY FAIR (MEADVILLE)
1848-2022

"The largest agricultural county fair east of the Mississippi River"

The very first Crawford County Fair held in 1848, featured a mere 10 entries of sheep and hogs on the main floor and needlecrafts on the second floor. The fairs continued from 1849-1861 before interruption due to the Civil War.

Six years later, the fair resumed but had to be relocated because so many buildings had been destroyed during the war.

In 1946, a contract was signed to rebuild and relocate the half-mile racetrack that had been built at a cost of $8,000. In 1947, construction included a grandstand, a horse barn and pole shelter for $9,500; a new display building for $10,000; an additional pole building for $2,300; a new restroom; a show arena; a youth building, and a race secretary's office.

In order to get to the announcer's booth you must climb a catwalk from the back to the front of the grandstand --- a total of about 76 steps. Demanding, perhaps, but race announcer Roger Huston has made that wearying walk every year.

Today, Crawford County Fair is still one of the best-attended fairs as people from neighboring counties travel to see such attractions as the Calf Scramble, Chicken Scramble, Sheep Scramble, Tractor Pull, Demo Derby, and of course, the most popular event, harness racing.

WAYNE COUNTY FAIR (Honesdale)
1849-2022

"Named after General Wayne"

Wayne County Fair is located in Honesdale, the northeast corner of Pennsylvania: 100 miles west of New York City, 150 miles north of Philadelphia and 35 miles east of Scranton/Wilkes-Barre.

In 1798, the county was formed and named after Revolutionary War General "Mad Anthony" Wayne. Today, the fair includes two large midways with over 26 rides, games, fantastic food and harness racing at its best.

On April 13, 1856, The Union Agricultural Society at Palmyra filed incorporation papers and held a three-day fair in October that year. In 1869, the Wayne County Agricultural Society introduced horse racing to the fair.

At the Wayne County Fair there are horse pulls, tractor pulls, truck pulls --- even a pony pull.

In 2010, Jeff Firmstone, race secretary and one of PA fair harness racing's best friends, offered horsemen a $500 bonus (pacer or trotter) if they broke the track's existing record in the free-for-all, which attracted many new horses. At that time, on the half-mile mile Honesdale oval, only a horse named *KT Beaner* (in 2003) had ever beaten 2:00, pacing in 1:59.4. *KT Beaner* was named after trainer Steve Schoeffel, whose nickname is Beaner.

GREAT ALLENTOWN FAIR
1852-2022

"Dan Patch sets a world record of 2:01 in 1905"

The Great Allentown Fair is one of the oldest fairs in the United States and one of the largest in Pennsylvania. The very first fair took place on Oct. 6, 1852, showcasing agricultural advancements and entertaining the town folk. The initial fair was so successful that in 1853, the society purchased a larger plot of land to expand.

Throughout the 1870s and 1880s, the popularity of the fair continued to grow. However, you can never make everybody happy, and the crowd was dissatisfied with the fairgrounds' size, short racetrack and grandstand. So in 1878, a plot of land was purchased and a new half-mile track was built with grandstands capable of seating 2,500 people. Thus, it became known as "The Great Allentown Fair."

In 1902, the fair's half-mile track was known as "one of the finest in the country" and lived up to it when in 1905 Dan Patch set a record in a remarkable time of 2:01.

In 1911, a 7,070-seat grandstand was constructed at a cost of $100,000 to host harness racing. Due to World War I, no fairs were held in 1917 and 1918, and the fairground was transformed into *Camp Crane,* a training facility for the U.S. Army Ambulance Service.

The fair was also absent between 1942 and 1945, but in 1951 General Douglas MacArthur, his wife, and son Arthur attended "Father and Son" day at the Allentown Fair; considered by many as "probably the most significant moments in the fair's history."

In the 1960s many celebrities such as Roy Rogers and Lawrence Welk appeared at the Great Allentown Fair, as did television host Johnny Carson. Other celebrities who graced the stage were Kiss, Styx, Alice Cooper, Taylor Swift, Yes, Lynyrd Skynyrd, Journey, Toby Keith, Bob Dylan and Rod Stewart.

Since the opening of the Great Allentown Fair, it has been visited by millions of people.

**"'Butler Comet Retirement Race
at the Bloomsburg Fair.
William Daugherty Jr. driving"**

BLOOMSBURG FAIR
1855-2022

"President Pierce and James Pollock persuaded 1,000 people to donate 10 cents each to launch the fair"

The Bloomsburg Fair, held in Bloomsburg, PA, was founded in 1855 when the 14th president of the United States, Franklin Pierce, and James Pollock, the 13th Governor of Pennsylvania, persuaded 1,000 people to donate ten cents each to launch the fair. Originally, it was held as an agricultural exhibition that took place on the lower end of Second Street but was relocated and is now located on Main Street.

Presumably, it began as a one-day production, but by 1857 it was running for two days. In 1858 until the late 1870s it became a three-day fair, and in 1892 it began operating full time as a three-day fair.

Besides harness racing, the Bloomsburg Fair provides high-end entertainment, such as country music featuring Lady Antebellum and Trace Adkins. It was at the Bloomsburg Fair that superstar Taylor Swift performed her very first major concert in front of a sellout crowd.

An assortment of carnival rides for the little and big ones; contests in baking, photography, canning, and the showing of farm animals are some of the amenities that draw thousands of people yearly to the fair. There's also a Farmers' Market --- a place where growers peddle homegrown vegetables and fruits.

And of course, there's harness racing. All races are one-mile dashes held for 2-year-old pacers and trotters (colt and filly divisions), 3-year-old trotters and pacers (colt and filly divisions), and sire stakes.

CLEARFIELD COUNTY FAIR
1861-2022

"*Stickler Hanover* sets a track record in 2020"

Although Clearfield was founded in 1805, the first fair didn't actually take place until 1861. In the early days, Clearfield was a big lumber town surviving because of its rich deposits of coal and clay. Clearfield was known as "the Pennsylvania town in the middle of nowhere" because of it's beauty, old-fashioned charm and heartwarming friendliness.

For 161 years, millions of people have visited the Clearfield County Fair to enjoy the food, activities, rides and harness racing.

The clay-based, half-mile track hosts a full card of pacers and trotters to an enthusiastic, packed grandstand. In 2020, the *Explosive Matter* colt, *Stickler Hanover,* trotted the fastest mile in the history of the fair in 2:01.1, breaking the mark set by *Bet On Tom* in 2017.

Today harness racing remains highly popular at the Clearfield County Fair. The fair lasts seven days, but it actually feels like three weeks because numerous parties are held throughout the week for crowds approaching up to a quarter-million people.

"Jimmy Stewart and Roger Huston at the Indiana County Fair"

"Indiana Fair"

INDIANA COUNTY FAIR
1862-2022

"Actor Jimmy Stewart's Birthplace"

Indiana County is located in the foothills of the Allegheny Mountains. It is a one-hour drive east of Pittsburgh, separated from Westmoreland and Allegheny counties by the act of March 12, 1803.

The Indiana County Fair was originally called 'The Indiana County Agricultural Society," and the harness racing circuit was known as "Coal, Iron and Oil Racing Circuit"—which embraced the best tracks, horses and meets.

When the fair opened in 1862, racehorses shipped in by express coaches to compete in the harness races. On Sept. 21, 1893,the headline in the *Indiana County Gazette* listed the horses and owners of the week's program. The scheduled races that day were *The Prospect Stake, The Mule Race, The County Trot, The Citizen Stake* and *The Speed Stakes*.

The major stables were Morning Side Farms, Sunny Side Farms and Cherry Tree Stock Farm and the individual owners were A.D. Sutton, N.G. Edelblute, P. Heffley, L.S. Hoyt, J.A. Quay, A.W. Harbison and S.S. Henderson.

On Aug. 17, 1909, a writer for *Horse World* praised the fair by saying, *It was the best half-mile track in the entire Keystone State. This is practically the home of Frank Jamison ---the clever Knight of the Sulky who has piloted many stars of the turf to victory.*

With a population of 8,000, Indiana was noted for its coalmines and rich farm country. Indiana County is home to a large Amish population, which has extensively grown to over 800 settlers since 1961.

Perhaps the most acclaimed fact about Indiana County --- it's the birthplace of actor Jimmy Stewart. It is also known as "The Christmas Tree Capital of the World."

Growing Christmas trees as a farm crop there started in 1918, and in 1956, an estimated 700,000 trees in Indiana were cut.

Ever since 1862, the Indiana County Fair has provided entertainment for the entire family. There are exhibits in livestock and contests for draft horses, swine, sheep, milk chugging, showmanship and log sawing.

GREENE COUNTY FAIR (WAYNESBURG) 1867-2022

"Is it a plane? Is it a bird? No, it's Birdman!"

The Greene County Fair/aka the Waynesburg Fair is one of only two county owned fairs in Pennsylvania, as the others is owned by shareholders.

At the Greene County Fair you can find livestock, home and garden exhibits, and horse racing. And you could also engage in gambling, which did not sit too well with the media that condemned it.

The fair shut down for several years in the early 1890s when the association was forced to dissolve and sell all property to pay for damages to Mary Elizabeth Wiley, who lost an eye in a shooting gallery accident.

By the mid 1890s the fair was taken over by a new organization, which quickly became quite popular --- allowing the illegal sale of beer or whiskey.

The fairgrounds sold again in 1901, and no fairs were held from 1901-1910.

In 1912, people from Greene County saw their first Air Show featuring "Birdman" Joe Stevenson, who delighted the crowd on opening day. Due to inclement weather the following day, "Birdman" crashed during takeoff; he was ejected from the plane and broke his collarbone.

THE GREAT STONEBORO FAIR
1868-2022

"J. T. Arturo and Roger Hammer set record in 2002"

In 1868, the Mercer County Agricultural Society of Stoneboro organized the very first fair, situated between noisy railroad tracks and a serene, scenic lake.

Due to the fair's instant popularity, the founding officers purchased 32 rolling acres two miles away from the original location and expanded it. The new site was much more appealing for it was now surrounded by shade trees that overlooked the town. The commission renamed it the Mercer Agricultural Society, but most still called it The Great Stoneboro Fair.

Soon after relocating, a half-mile racetrack was constructed that was used for harness racing, demolition derbies, truck and tractor pulls, and rodeos. The new track attracted talented drivers and horses from far away.

In 2002, The United States Trotting Association awarded Stoneboro the Blue Ribbon Award for having "the best harness racing program."

In 1986, a new track record for trotters was set by *Laser Almahurst* in 2:00.2 with driver Harold Brocklehurst.

The record for pacers was set in 2002 by *J. T. Arturo* in 1:57, with "The Hammer," Roger Hammer, in the bike.

LYCOMING FAIR
1870-2022

"In 1944 a severe thunderstorm destroyed the exhibition building"

The origin of the Lycoming Fair actually was in 1868, three years after the end of the American Civil War. Thrilled the war had ended, the townspeople looked to bring some excitement and fun to the town.

In 1870 the Muncy Valley Farmers Club held its first exhibition where people could bring livestock, fruits, vegetables, canned goods and handicrafts. Over the years the fair thrived.

The Muncy Valley Farmers' Club grew its membership to nearly 200 by 1875, and a charter of incorporation was drawn up. Dues were set at 50 cents per year.

In the 1920s, automobile racing on the dirt track drew massive crowds due to the economic "good times" of the "Roaring Twenties." The popularity of the automobile encouraged people to travel and they started attending the fair. But the Lycoming Fair was curtailed starting in 1942 due to restrictions and demands of World War II.

Tragedy struck the fairgrounds on Sept. 4, 1944, during a severe thunderstorm when a large exhibition building was hit by lightning, destroying the structure.

In the 1950s, the date for the fair was changed from when it originally opened (usually September or October) to mid-July, and the fair was extended to 10 days.

"Tony and Todd Schadel at their hometown fair in Gratz"

GRATZ FAIR
1873-2022

"Roger Hammer --the King of the Fairs -- survives accident"

Every year since 1873, a fair has been held in the county of Dauphin in the town of Gratz. The fair is a beloved stop on the PA fair circuit that has been delighting horsemen, participants and spectators for 134 years.

On Dec. 15,1873, a petition was submitted to the county court for a charter, marking the beginning of the Gratz Driving Park (as it was known at that time). D.M. Romberger, an enterprising businessman, initiated a stagecoach run to carry fair-goers from Millersburg to Gratz each day. The cost for the round trip was $1.50.

For the first several years, profits were marginal, but over the next few years they steadily increased. Unfortunately, there were a few unexpected setbacks, such as a devastating snowstorm in December 1891 that destroyed all the stables and sheds on the fairgrounds. To enhance income, fair directors decided to rent parcels of the grounds to farmers, so long as they agreed to grow only grass that could be harvested into hay.

In 1907 the board decided to sell the fairgrounds for $2,000 at a public auction: the highest bid of $1,900 was declined. A week later the grounds were sold for $2,000 and a new team gained control, appointing Harry Smith president.

Smith made many changes and improvements, such as adding a variety of new amusement rides along with more emphasis on harness racing.

In 1901, a half-mile track was constructed and new stables and a new grandstand were built.

The year 1901 was considered a banner year for "high-class trotting horses;" one of the races that day was won by *Davis Wise's Dutch* in a time of 2:25.1.

In 2003, Roger Hammer drove trotter *Shark Kosmos* to a track record 1:58.2. When the duo returned for a '"free-for-all" event the following year, a horse in front of *Shark Kosmos* got tangled in his hopples, went down, and flipped the trailing Hammer from the bike. Hammer finally freed the lines as his colt was tearing across the grounds. Finally stopping between two cars in the parking lot, *Shark Kosmos* was miraculously unscathed.

Unfortunately, Hammer wasn't as lucky and was flown to a local hospital where he was diagnosed with a dislocated shoulder, a broken shoulder blade and several broken ribs. Although Hammer was sidelined for eight weeks, it was impossible to keep "The Hammer" down and he was soon back.

In 2004, Todd Schadel's pacer, *Shu Hanover,* surprised even his owner, winning in 1:56.2 while setting a new track record.

In 2009, the 2-year-old Arturo pacer, *DVC Givemeattitude,* set a new track record of 1:58.2 --- his 11th win that year. The colt was owned, trained and driven by Dave Brickell.

Hammer and Schadel --- co-owners of the 2005 Hambletonian *Vivid Photo* --- are permanent fixtures at the Gratz Fair.

One year, Race Secretary Don Wiest bought a raffle ticket at the fair -- the prize was a peafowl of undetermined gender. Wiest won. After Wiest discovered that his prize fowl was a male peacock, a friend located a female. Soon the two birds do what a male and female of the species do best ---- produce lots of little peafowl.

BEDFORD COUNTY FAIR
1874-2022

"Like father, like son. Clay and Roger Hammer rule the Bedford Fair"

The English town of Bedford has an interesting history. Founded by the Danes on March 9, 1771, Bedford was recaptured by the English King Edward in 915 A.D.

The Normans built a wooden castle to keep the people in order, but in 1224 a rebellious baron held the castle against the king and destroyed it.

In the Middle Ages, Bedford had a weekly market and an annual fair; in 1554 Bedford was permitted to have two annual fairs. Horsemen would drive 40 miles, bringing their horses to Bedford to race by train or hitched to a buggy.

In 1909, Bedford joined a new racing circuit called "The Central Pennsylvania" that included fairground tracks in Altoona, Tyrone, Huntingdon, Hollidaysburg, Clearfield, Carroltown, Myersdale and Bellefonte. Of these, only Bedford, Clearfield and Myersdale continue to conduct races today.

In 1925, the fair association hired an engineer to design an official U.S.T.A. half-mile track over the existing track; it wouldn't be built until 1936.

The early horse barns lined the north side of the fairgrounds property, with the barns creating a perimeter barn. In the late 1950s a local group built new stables in the woods on the southwest corner of the grounds and remained there 60 years until a group of 4-H leaders raised funds and built two new barns, replacing those built in the 1950s.

The Bedford County Fair is located in beautiful south-central Pennsylvania and provides fun and amenities for people of all ages.

Through the years the fair has hosted its share of premier drivers and horses. One notable was Clay Hammer, who won his share of races, while his son Roger who is considered "the king of the fair circuit" today. In 2005, Roger and *Vivid Photo* shocked the racing world by coming from far back to win the prestigious Hambletonian.

Another Bedford County boy who has made good in racing is Sam Beegle and his Ginger Tree Farms Stable.

Over the past seven decades many horsemen have made a living racing horses at Bedford County while for others it is a fun hobby.

"Grand Circuit Races --- Philadelphia 1917"

THE BELMONT DRIVING PARK
1876- 1924

Although an actual fair was never held at The Belmont Driving Park in Philadelphia, Grand Circuit races were. The Belmont Driving Park was the gathering place for sulky horse racing and its devoted fans in the late 1800s and early 1900s.

A mile-long oval track for harness racing was created in 1876 on land called Price's Field. This is the site where George Washington and his troops camped on Sept. 13, 1777.

In 1890, a half-mile track was built within the original oval, and the clubhouse was an elaborate three-story building with wide verandas and a second-floor porch.

Dressed in their finest outfits and shaded by delicate parasols, ladies sipped lemonade as men cheered the sulky races from porches below.

Horse racing was extremely popular, and favorite horses such as *Star Pointer, The Guideless Wonder, Jay Eye See, May Queen* and *Maude S. Smuggler* were some of the featured stars.

For the Grand Circuit of 1917, pacers and trotters came by train from stables in New Hampshire, Kentucky, Ohio and Massachusetts, arriving at the Cynwyd Rail Station.

In the fall of 1924, the entire acreage was sold to a construction company for $300,000 (an astounding 200 percent profit for the stockholders). With plans for 374 lots, paved streets, sidewalks and a number of fine homes, Merion Park became a substantial residential community where, sadly, many of its homeowners never even heard of the exciting sulky races of the past.

SOMERSET COUNTY FAIR
1900-2022

"Harness racing resumes after a 50-year hiatus"

The history, traditions and legends of Somerset County are colorful threads interwoven in the evolving pattern of American Civilization. Historically speaking, Somerset County, about 70 miles southeast of Pittsburgh, is young, even in a new world.

Although it took decades, after 50 years harness racing finally returned to enthusiastic fans. The county fair board was the driving force behind the rebirth of the sport, although much work needed done, such as upgrading the track, which until then had been used for demolition derbies and truck pulls.

With expert advice and guidance from horsemen Rich Gillock and Sam Beegle, the track was reconstructed, emerging wider than the old surface, allowing six horses to race across.

In 2021, harness races were streamed live from the Somerset County Fair, showing the entire 10 race card.

A yearly Somerset County event for over 100 years, this eight-day agricultural and educational fair features carnival rides, games, entertainment, an exhibit hall, animal shows and judging, competitions, delicious food and harness racing.

CHAPTER THREE

Pennsylvania Harness Racing

"The Original Meadows Racing Program"

BRANDYWINE RACEWAY

Known as "one of the prettiest racetracks ever built," picturesque Brandywine Raceway was surrounded by trees and lush greenery. Opening night at Brandywine Raceway was Sept.7, 1953, drawing 14,182 enthusiastic fans.

Although Brandywine was not actually located in Pennsylvania proper, it was just over the southern border of Pennsylvania at south Philadelphia.

Brandywine was originally a top-tier half-mile harness track located in Wilmington, DE but was converted to a five-eighths-mile venue in 1960. It was Brandywine that introduced metropolitan Philadelphians to harness racing.

When Liberty Bell opened in 1963 it became, with Brandywine, a circuit, as the two Delaware Valley tracks would not compete against each other.

For years Brandywine, combined with Liberty Bell Park, produced a circuit that was second only to the Yonkers-Roosevelt circuit. Unfortunately, the two tracks eventually turned on each other and ran conflicting events, sadly leading to the demise of both.

Rick Kane, the race secretary today at The Downs at Mohegan Sun Pocono, acted as race secretary at Brandywine in 1987-1988. His memories of Brandywine are heartfelt: *Brandywine Raceway was one of the most beautiful harness tracks ever built, and the history is limitless.*

LIBERTY BELL PARK
1963-1986

"Liberty Bell drew all the best drivers and horses"

Liberty Bell Park, a racetrack located in northeast Philadelphia, held both harness and Thoroughbred racing from 1963-1986.

Located just off the Pennsylvania Turnpike and minutes away from Exit 6 on the New Jersey Turnpike, it was accessible for prominent stables like the Dancers and the Haughtons to race at Liberty Bell instead of Yonkers or Roosevelt Raceway.

The harness track was five-eighths miles, but when Thoroughbred racing was legalized in 1968, a one-mile track was built using the homestretch and front of the harness track, and in 1974, Keystone Race Track was built on the other side of the Pennsylvania Turnpike to accommodate Thoroughbreds.

Liberty Bell offered a glass-enclosed facility that provided seating for 10,000 while the clubhouse seated 5,500. It was estimated the facility could accommodate a total of 30,000.

On June 8,1963, opening night at Liberty Bell, *Majesty's Knight* won the initial pari-mutuel race. That opening card was highlighted by the $20,000 Liberty Bell Pace, which was split in two divisions for 3-year-old colts.

The first division was won by *Max Hanover* and driven by the great Billy Haughton; "The Super Horse," *Overtrick,* won the second division for John Patterson. That was the start of Liberty Bell becoming a premier harness track on the East Coast.

Although that night brought in $476,818, it was a slight disappointment, for it was below the projected break-even point of $500,000.

During that first 49-day season in 1963, Liberty Bell Park's success made it "one of the main harness tracks on the East Coast," helping the sport reach record-breaking highs in attendance and pari-mutuel handle.

In 1965, the Hanover Stakes began, although at that time they never went for big money. In 1968, Thoroughbred racing was authorized in Pennsylvania, but there was no place to stage the races, so three Pennsylvania tracks, including The Meadows and Pocono Downs, came to the rescue, taking on the Thoroughbred meets.

Liberty Bell constructed a mile oval around the existing oval, with both breeds using the same stretch. After the Pennsylvania Racing Commission declared that each breed must run at separate tracks, Thoroughbred racing lasted only five more years at Liberty Bell. Once Thoroughbreds returned to Keystone Race Track, Liberty Bell reverted exclusively to harness racing.

Many famous horses competed at Liberty Bell in the 1960s and 1970s, such as: *Nevele Pride, Columbia George, Super Bowl, Yankee Bambino, Strike Out, Green Speed, Flak Bait, Romulus Hanover, Nero, Overtrick, Meadow Skipper, Nansemond, Albatross* and *Windshield Wiper.*

The opening of the Meadowlands in 1976 drew away many of Liberty Bell's top drivers and horses. When the refurbished Garden State Park (located on the other side of the Ben Franklin Bridge) began conducting harness racing, the elite drivers and horses remained in New Jersey.

Today, the site of what was one of the nicest harness tracks in Pennsylvania is now the Franklin Mills Mall.

INTERESTING FACTS ABOUT LIBERTY BELL PARK

1963: *Majesty's Knight* wins first pari-mutuel.

1967: A record crowd of 22,989 attends.

1971: An all-time record is set when $1,616,89 is wagered on the evening's card.

1974: Liberty Bell returns to harness racing.

1985: Liberty Bell closes its doors.

"The Meadows Family"

"Delvin Miller and Adios"

"Dragon's Lair and Jeff Mallet win the Breeders Crown at The Meadows""

"1983 --- Delvin Miller Celebrates Adios Week with friends: Boots Randolph, Delvin Miller, Eddie Rabbitt, Chet Atkins, Bob Prince, Mr. Coffee, and Joe DiMaggio"

HOLLYWOOD CASINO AT THE MEADOWS

HOLLYWOOD CASINO AT THE MEADOWS
1963 --

"Home of the celebrated Adios"

I guess you could say I'm biased when talking about The Meadows, now known as Hollywood Casino at The Meadows, located in Washington, PA, for that is where it all began for me.

My greatest thrills in harness racing have taken place there, for which I will always be thankful. Therefore, when I was asked to write a book on the history of harness racing in the Keystone State, I was humbled and quite honored. For me to be able to give back to the sport and people that have been a major part of my life is fulfilling.

Change is hard, and we can't do anything about it but go with the flow. I have seen so many changes in the sport since I first got involved 45 years ago: some good and some not so good. But for me, harness racing is still the most exciting game in town, and the horse is one of God's greatest creations.

The Meadows is a wonderful place to race your horses. and the people are dedicated, kind and hard working. Many champions --- both two-and four-legged --- call, or have called The Meadows home, such as icons Delvin Miller, Ed Ryan, Dick Stillings, Dave Palone, Pete Cameron, Joe Hardy, The Burke Brigade and Roy Davis.

Multiple world records were set at The Meadows, the most recent being the 1:47.1 turned in by *Papi Rob Hanover* in 2020.

Local horseman Dave Palone is the "winningest" driver in harness history while Meadows-based Ron Burke boasts the same honor among trainers.

I was blessed to be there when my friend, trainer/driver Dick Stillings, won the 1986 Adios with one of his "Spur" boys. The grandstand was packed as everyone cheered for the local horseman and his horse owned by Roy Davis. In eye-catching purple, the traditional color for The Adios, a blanket of orchids was placed over *Barberry Spur's* back. With that victory, *Barberry Spur* became the first locally connected horse to ever win The Adios.

Families such as the Altmeyers, Beinhauers, Snyders, Parkers, Bolons, Piatts, Dunns, Stillings, Harveys, Provosts, Hammers, Zendts, and Burkes continue to help in keeping The Meadows as one of the nation's leading harness tracks.

As other celebrated tracks have been shut down, The Meadows has overcome the odds and survived.

"Dreams Can Come True"

A dream is a series of ideas, emotions and images that occur in the mind. Everyone has them, but not everyone has the tenacity and willpower to make dreams come true.

The great American animator Walt Disney once said, *"If you can dream it, you can do it."*

Well, that is exactly what driver, trainer, owner and the "Ambassador of Harness Racing" Delvin Miller did on June 28, 1963.

Miller's vision of bringing the best harness racing to fans would come to fruition when the doors initially opened at his new state-of-the-art "baby," The Meadows. Since that day, The Meadows has been a leader in innovations that have kept racing strong.

It was 1959 when Pennsylvania legalized racehorse wagering. Several years later, voters of Allegheny County defeated a referendum to open a harness track so Delvin Miller and the Washington Trotting Association purchased land 25 miles south of Pittsburgh and converted it into The Meadows.

November of 1962 was cold and snowy, but that didn't deter Miller and his fellow pioneers from breaking ground to build the first pari-mutuel horse racing track in Western Pennsylvania.

After overcoming many obstacles, the doors opened for gambling and entertainment on June 28, 1963. A total of 7,641 spectators showed up to watch the inaugural program.

Opening night featured a nine-race card, including a $14,000 Arden Downs stake in which horseman Dick Wood took the honors with *Wee Crusader.*

At this time racetracks were constructed of only dirt, sand and turf. The "Innovator," The Meadows, set new standards when it opted for a synthetic carpet made of a newly minted mixture called "Tartan Turf." It was the first of its kind, and as anything new, it had its skeptics.

Tartan Turf was expensive, but Miller saw a surface that was impervious to the elements, reducing the risk of injuries and saving maintenance costs.

Previous winter testing, conducted at Max Hempt's training facility in central Pennsylvania, indicated the synthetic mixture could withstand the inclement winter weather in western Pennsylvania.

After 10 years of horsemen complaining about coming back mud-splattered and clobbered with clumps of dirt, the Tartan Track was replaced in 1975 with the "lightning" limestone surface that is still in use today.

In 1967 Miller launched what would become The Meadows signature race, *The Adios*. The race for three-year-old pacers was named after Delvin's pride and joy, his foundation sire, *Adios.*

Every year top drivers and trainers across North America compete in The Adios, also known as the "Pace of the Orchids." Hall of Famers Billy Haughton, Stanley Dancer, Joe O'Brien, Ron Pierce and John Campbell all have won The Adios, Campbell a record eight times.

The Meadows was also a great place to be at in the morning hours. The track kitchen was always crowded, for not only did the chef provide the best food for horsemen, but you also never knew who would walk in. Occasionally Miller (carrying a putter) would come with his '"friends" — Arnold Palmer, Whitey Ford, Jay Silverheels, or Canonsburg native, singer Perry Como.

Another happening place at The Meadows was the famous Hill located behind he track kitchen. At that time children were not allowed in the grandstand, so families would sit on the Hill, cheering on their horse.

On Adios Day people would mark their spot with blankets they placed the night before; at times there could easily be 500 people scattered across the Hill.

On Oct. 11, 1971, a Thoroughbred meet scheduled to last 67 days commenced. In 1972 the meet took place, but due to poor weather and a dismal handle, management opted to close down the meet early.

In 1974, The Meadows was sold to Global Development, Inc. of Washington, PA. The new ownership group invested $1.5 million in track improvements, adding barns, enclosing the grandstand, and resurfacing the five-eighths-mile track.

The legacy of The Meadows continues as healthy purses create exciting, competitive racing and where four Harness Racing Hall of Famers --- Roger Huston, Dave Palone, Ron Burke and Dick Stillings still call home.

Thank you Delvin Miller, for having a dream and making it come true.

Without you there would be no Meadows. You are truly a Superstar.

INTERESTING FACTS ABOUT THE MEADOWS

1948: Delvin Miller, " The Ambassador of Harness Racing," establishes Meadow Lands Farm in Pennsylvania as a home for his horse Adios, who would become the leading sire in the history of the sport.

1963:Pari-mutuel racing is legalized in Pennsylvania.

1967: The first Adios Pace is contested with *Romulus Hanover* winning the final heat in 1:57.3. The purse is $85,510.

1983:The Meadows Racing Network broadcasts its first show from a semi-enclosed booth. Roger Huston and guest analyst Jerry Connors are the hosts. (Ironically, I was the first female co-host --- a time I will never forget.)

1984: *Dragon's Lair*, trained and driven by Pittsburgh's own Jeff Mallet, upsets the favored *Nihilator* in the Breeders Crown for 2-year-old colt and gelding pacers.

1986: Tyler Stillings becomes the youngest co-host to appear with Huston on the televised show. That night the Stillings/Goldberg stable had *OK* Eric in the final of the Royal Travel Pacing Series. The horse wins, and Stillings left the booth to go the winners' circle. Jokingly Huston announces, *My co-host has left the building.*

Mid-1990's: Due to competition from slot machines, The Meadows attendance declines.

1995: The Meadows becomes the home of the Messenger Stakes, one of the legs of harness racing's Triple Crown.

1999: The Hilton Group PLC (parent firm of Ladbroke USA) puts The Meadows Racetrack up for sale.

2001: Magna Entertainment acquires The Meadows.

2008: "The Voice," Meadows announcer Roger Huston, calls his 150,000th race.

2009: The fastest triple-dead-heat in harness racing history goes in the books as *TSM Goldenridge, Serious Damage* and *Teen Elvis* cross the line so closely the camera can't separate them. The race goes in 1:53.4.

(In 2015, that record is eclipsed by a trio of pacers at Saratoga who dead-heat in 1:52.2 --- in the slop, no less.)

2012: Palone gets victory 15,181, making him the all-time "winningest" driver in North American harness history. In the winning circle the great Herve Filion, whose record is eclipsed, congratulates Palone.

2015: Penn National Gaming's parent company acquires The Meadows and rebrands it Hollywood Casino at The Meadows.

2020: *Papi Rob Hanover* sets a world record of 1:47.1, the fastest mile ever recorded on a five-eighths-mile track.

"Dick Stillings and Barberry Spur Win The Adios"

‘The Meadows Celebrates 50 Years””

“Meadows drivers”

“Adios wearing Steeler blanket”

THE DOWNS AT MOHEGAN SUN POCONO

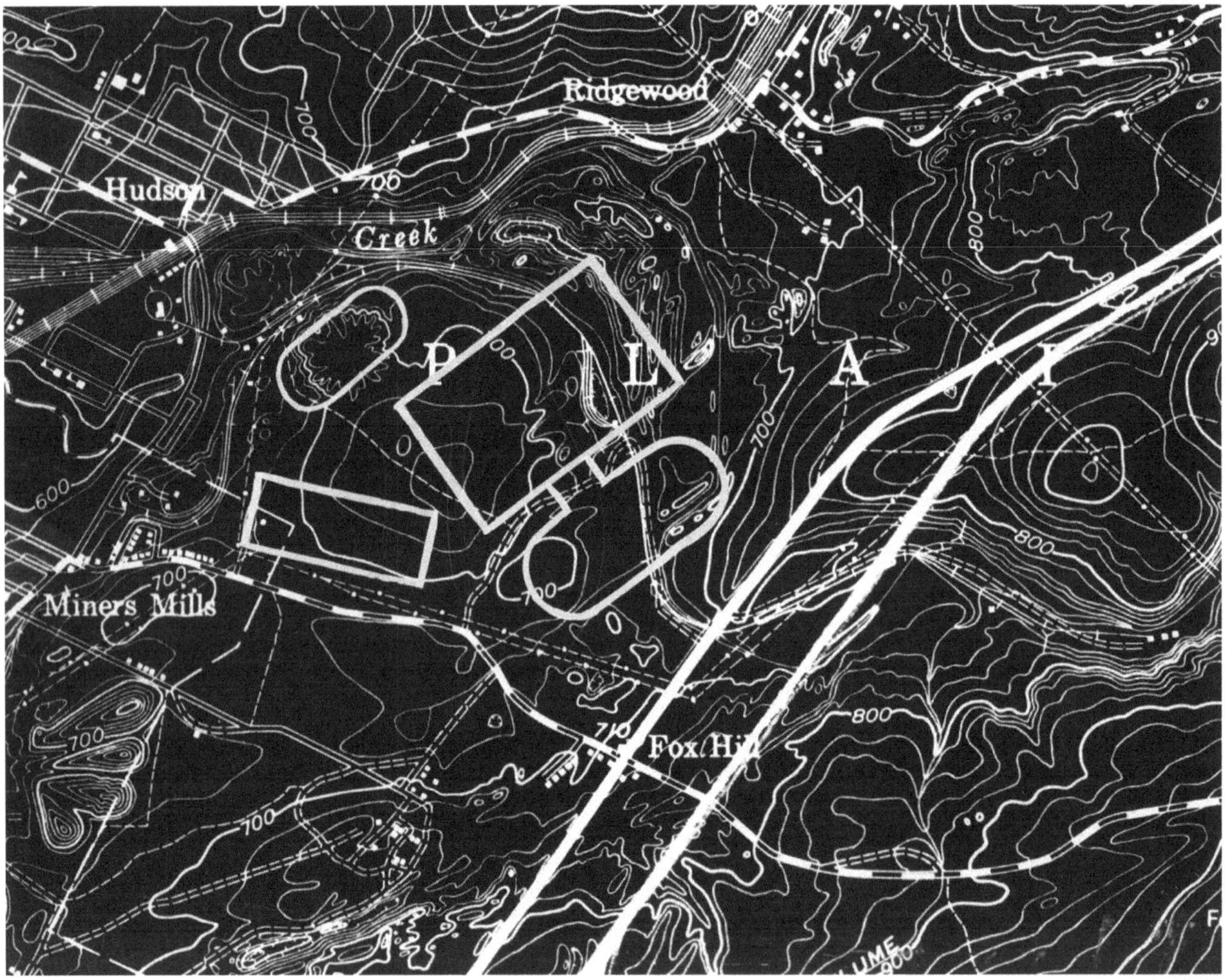

"Aerial Blueprint of Pocono Downs before the track was formed"

"Aerial Photo of Pocono Downs"

THE DOWNS AT MOHEGAN SUN POCONO
1965 ---

"The Magic Red Clay"

Pocono Downs, now known as The Downs At Mohegan Sun Pocono, is near Wilkes-Barre. Located on 400 acres on the hillside of Plains, PA, it is within easy access of New York, Philadelphia, New Jersey and Delaware.

Pocono's five-eighths-mile oval is acknowledged as "one of the best track surfaces in America." Every year Pocono hosts major harness stakes, such as the Max Hempt Memorial Pace and the Reynolds Stakes.

It all started on July 15,1965 when the doors opened to a crowd of approximately 12,000 fans --- all there to see "the new kid on the block" join its racing neighbors, Liberty Bell Park to the south and The Meadows to the west.

Pocono immediately became one of northeastern Pennsylvania's top attractions, drawing spectators from hundreds of miles away. By all accounts horse racing was a thrilling evening and the first of many to come.

The founding fathers of Pocono Downs were James and Anna Jean Durkin. Durkin, a one-time president of the Great American Coal Company was a partner of Fred Correale, a reputed member of the Buffalino northeastern Pennsylvania crime family.

The completion of the track cost an estimated $7 million. A five-eighths-mile oval with a surface of a stone-aggregate base largely composed of stone dust with red rock screenings in the top layer was constructed, thus giving the appearance a reddish color, unlike most harness tracks.

The grandstand could accommodate 3,000, the clubhouse up to 500, and the stables housed up to 900 horses.

The first winner of that initial season was *Satin Queen*; the track record for trotters was by *Singing Arrow* in 2:02.2, and *Heineken* took the honors for pacers, winning in 2:00.4.

In 1967, Pocono would see its first "Magic Mile" as driver Clarence Martin, Sr. guided *Scarlet Wave* to a 1:59.4 triumph.

In 1996, the track's parent company purchased Pocono for $47 million from the estate of the late Joseph B. Banks. In 2005, the track was once again sold as Mohegan Sun acquired Pocono from Penn National Gaming for $280 million and renamed it Mohegan Sun at Pocono Downs.

Immediately the new owners began a major expansion, renovating the grandstand area with two floors of slot machines, office space, a food court and a new simulcast area.

In 1972, Mother Nature came to town and played a dirty trick on Wilkes-Barre when Hurricane Agnes made an unwanted appearance, flooding the streets and devastating the town. The track played a significant role acting as an evacuation and distribution center, logistical headquarters, and a mobile medical facility --- all at the same time.

A call came in for empty feedbags to be filled with sand to reinforce the valley's defenses; the horsemen provided those bags and converted the clubhouse to an infirmary and registration center staffed by 20 volunteer nurses.

Dr. Mario Sindaco, the track's physician who had his home swept away by the flood, organized medical corps of volunteers tending to evacuees, while the more seriously injured were transported to Wilkes-Barre General Hospital or the VA Hospital.

In the barn area horsemen, both grooms and trainers, pitched in to help those hit the hardest, and track staff prepared food for those left homeless by "The Wrath of Agnes." The racetrack was part of the unsuccessful fight to hold back the Susquehanna River's raging waters.

One thing about harness racing is that during a crisis horsemen will pull together, leaving the racetrack rivalry on the back burner.

In the early 2000s, Pocono Downs fell on difficult times as tracks in neighboring states began reinventing themselves as "racinos." Things looked bleak until 2004 when Pennsylvania legislators voted to allow slot machines.

Many world records were set over the lightning red clay through the years. It took eight years before the track saw its first world record when 2-year-old trotting filly, *Starlark Hanover* with driver David Wade, would be the first. The time of 2:01 stood for eight years.

In 2013, a Maryland pacing-bred trotter named *Googoo Gaagaa* was victorious in the Beal Trot, stopping the timer in 1:50.4, and in 2014, *Sebastian K* with Ake Svanstedt in the bike, set an astonishing world record in 1:49.3.

As for the pacers, it was in 1969 when *Laverne Hanover* and Bill Haughton stopped the clock in a scintillating 1:56.3. In 2013, *Foiled Again*, the world's richest harness horse, swept the Ben Franklin Pace in 1:49.2, and in 2011 *Sweet Lou* paced the fastest mile by a 2 year-old, winning the Breeders Crown in 1:49.

Today, Pocono is owned and operated by the Mohegan Tribe of Connecticut.

INTERESTING FACTS ABOUT POCONO

1963: Ground is broken for construction of the new facility. When completed it would cost a whopping $7 million.

1965: The ribbon is cut and Pocono is off and racing. *Satin Queen* becomes the first horse to grace Pocono's Victory Lane.

1967: Pocono's sees it first "Magic Mile" when *Scarlet Wave* and driver Clarence Martin, Sr. wins in 1:59.4.

1969: Two-year-old pacer, *Laverne Hanover,* driven by Bill Haughton, stops the clock in 1:56.3.

1972: Flooding from Hurricane Agnes hits, devastating the grounds and surroundings. The racetrack is closed to help aid victims.

1973: *Starlark Hanover* sets a world record for two-year-old trotting fillies on a 5/8-mile track.

1977: The first "triple dead-heat" takes place as *Jeff Crain, Bootys Dizzy,* and *Royal Grant* cross the finish line together.

1988: A bill authorizing "track-run-but off-track betting parlors" is passed by the Legislature, and Pocono Downs first exports its racing signal to other racetracks.

1996: Pocono Downs is sold by the estate of Joseph Banks to Penn National Gaming Inc.

1998: Bill Lambertus wins the final of his co-record eight dash-winning driving titles.

2006: Pennsylvania's first casino opens at *Mohegan Sun at Pocono Downs*, with 1099 slot machines, a newly renovated Simulcast room, and a casual dining food court.

2009: The opening of the all-weather enclosed paddock with sufficient room to accommodate 14 races opens. It is the most modern of racehorse-related accouterments equipped with a sophisticated heating/cooling system.

2010: The Breeders Crown Championships are held at Pocono for the very first time, and the betting handle exceeds $2.3 million. This is also the year that table games make their Pocono and Pennsylvania debut.

2011: Two–year-old pacer *Sweet Lou* wins the Breeders Crown in 1:49.

2012: Three-year-old trotter *Googoo Gaagaa,* trained by Richard Hans and driven by Corey Callahan, wins the Simpson Stake in 1:50.4.

2013: The Breeders Crown Championships return to Pocono, with $3.2 million wagered worldwide.

2013: The worlds' richest horse, *Foiled Again,* trained by Ron Burke and driven by Yannick Gingras, wins the Breeders Crown at Pocono in 1:49.2 over a sloppy track.

2014: Trotter *Sebastian K* driven and trained by Ake Svanstedt, sets a new world record in 1:49. This was only the horse's fourth North American start.

2014: *Sweet Lou* sets a new world record in 1:47, the fastest time ever on a 5/8-mile track. He's trained by Ron Burke and driven by the great Ron Pierce.

Throughout various years Pocono has had three of the 25 triple dead-heats in the recorded history of harness racing ---more than any other North American harness track. They are:

POCONO'S FIRST: July 12, 1977
*BOOTY'S DIZZY (*Jim Fortna*), ROYAL GRANT (*Peter "Piker" Parolari*)* and *JEFF CRAIN (*Anthony Montegna*)* cross the wire in a dead-heat.

POCONO'S SECOND: May 13, 1980
FULLA PROMISE (Clarence Hand), *QUITE GUY* (Dominic Marusco) and *RON ((*Ralph Figlow) finish together in 2:05.

POCONO'S THIRD: Oct. 16, 1998
*HIGH PRESSURE (*Kevin Sizer), *BULLVILLE KENYA* (Rodney LaFramboise) and *INFECTIOUS LAUGH* (Bryce Truitt) finish as the camera proves them inseparable in the time of 1:57.

"Pocono Downs Family #1"

"Pocono Downs Family #2"

HARRAH'S PHILADELPHIA CASINO & RACETRACK

HARRAH'S PHILADELPHIA CASINO & RACETRACK 2006 –

"First Harness Track To Have a Casino"

Harrah's Philadelphia Casino & Racetrack is both a harness track and casino, (aka *racino*) owned by Vici Properties and operated by Caesar's Entertainment.

On Sept. 27, 2006, the Pennsylvania Gaming Control Board gave Harrah's its slots license; thus opening day for the modern facility was Jan. 22, 2007.

A total of 10,000 fans showed up. Barry Brown, director of racing operations, said, *It was the largest crowd we ever had or ever will have.*

The track was built on the site of the former Sun Shipbuilding campus. The five-eighths-mile racetrack consists of a limestone-based surface, and the paddock holds up to 131 horses, as many are shipped in.

Both the track and casino are on a 64-acre brownfield site that had been cleaned up and constructed after shipbuilding closed down in 1989.

The track was designed by the Coon Brothers from Kentucky who specialize in building horse ovals. The Coons designed the track partially over the water from the shipyard's wet dock, saying, *I can't think of a racetrack where you look out over the backstretch and see the water. It's very striking.*

Harrah's Philadelphia currently runs from early April to mid-December, and the racing broadcast at Harrah's is available via simulcast from other racetracks throughout the United States and Canada.

If you are looking for an awesome experience, Harrah's Philadelphia is the place to be. Thrilling harness racing, a vibrant nightlife, great food, and casino entertainment await you.

INTERESTING FACTS ABOUT HARRAH'S PHILADELPHIA

2006: There are multiple track records throughout the year.

2007 – 2013: James Witherite is the track announcer.

2014 – Present: Michael Bozich serves as track announcer.

PHOTO GALLERY

Herman Hylkema steers Von Baron pacing gelding Italian Lover to a fast training mile

"Herman Hylkema steers Italian Lover"

"Aime Choquette, Delvin Miller and Tom Charters"

"Stanley Dancer"

"Helen Pyle – The first Parade Marshall at The Meadows"

“Horsemen watching the races from the hill’”

“Greg Wasiluk, Race Secretary Phil Wentworth and Bobby Williams: Top dash winners 1982”

A Lifetime of Faith & Love

A Legacy of Happiness

Edward Martin Ryan Sr.

March 2nd, 1924 – June 1st, 2012

"Ed Ryan: Owner of The Meadows"

We're all Winners!

Thanks for the memories!
John Salvi & Damascus - 1972
Nick Salvi & Walkin Boots - 1969
"Life is a series of choices..."

CONGRATULATIONS TO THE WINNERS!
The Meadows & Harry & Trudy Sowash

In Memory of Harry, Janet, Patty &
Jerry Sowash & Everett Calvert - owner

The Sowash Family

GILLOCK STABLES

IRON CITY SMITTY, RALPH, KEITH, MIKE SR ,
MIKE, JAKE & RICH GILLOCK
50 YEARS OF RACING AT THE MEADOWS

Cecil Champion
1969

In memory of Jack Harrison.
Cecil & Frances Champion and
congratulations on 50 years from the rest of
The Harrison Family

JOE HUTCHISON

Frank & Sallee Hutchison
Raker

Rick & Kirsten Stillings
Sophia & Ella

Todd & Jenny Raker
Tyler & Trevor

" A MAN FOR ALL SEASONS"

"We're All Winners"

“Carol Ross—Meadows Parade Marshall at The Meadows”

"Dr. Wesley Parry"

"**Dr. Barry Betts**"

"Brooke Nickells Sets New Record Under Saddle at The Meadows"

"Mickey Burke Sr., Ron Burke and Evan Pattak"

“Harry Harvey (manager of Meadow Lands Farm) with New York Yankee pitcher Ralph Terry and Jockey Eddie Arcaro”

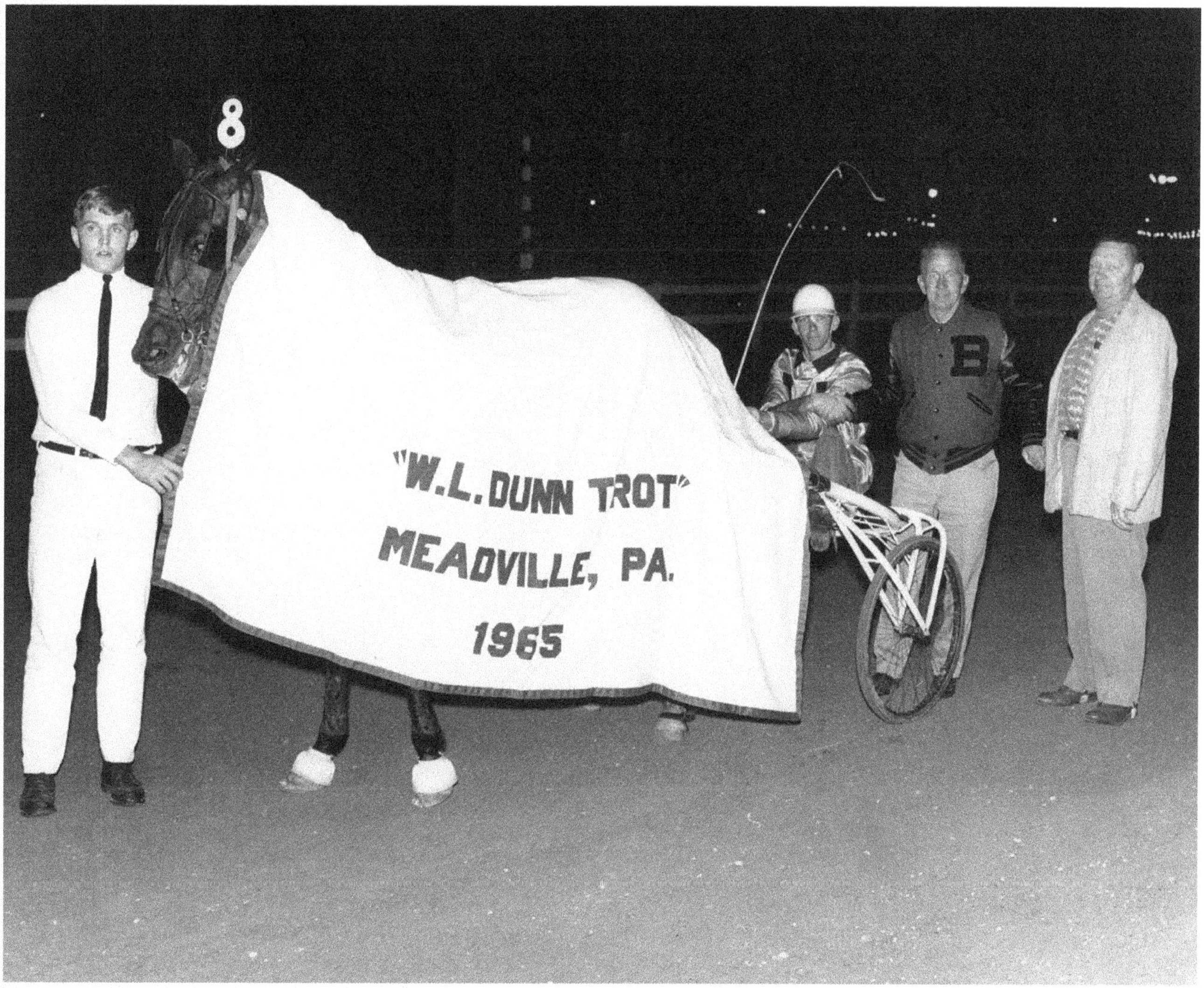

"Bill Daugherty wins W.L. Dunn Trot – Meadville Fair 1965"

“Bill Fahy and Jennas Beach Boy”

"Curby Stillings, Quinton Patterson and Ruby Cook"

BOOK TWO

"It Takes A Village"

"Meadows Race Secretaries"

"Joe DeFrank, Bill Connors, Ken Marshall, Tom Charters, Charlie Bishop, Gary Buxton and Tom Leasure."

PRESENT DAY HORSE RACING

Since harness racing began in the 1800s, much has changed. For one, technological advances in the horse racing industry have revolutionized the sport by modernizing the rules and traditions.

Modification of equipment and race bikes enables horses to go much faster than before, and the surface of the racetracks made from stone dust or red clay helps reduce the number of fatal injuries suffered by horses and drivers.

But probably the most significant reason horses are going faster is the purification of their gait. Fifty years ago, many horses were sired by double- gaited stallions who were capable of producing both pacers and trotters. Nowadays, it's nearly impossible to find a horse with double-gaited blood within five generations of their extended pedigrees. Consequently, pacers pace and trotters trot.

Today, given the purification of the horses' gait, trotters are capable of going a mile approaching 1:50, whereas years ago trotters seldom broke the 2:00 barrier. If you had a trotter go in 2:00, you had a good one. These days, pacers have stopped the clock in a mind-bending 1:46, and in 2022 that time was lowered to 1:45.4.

Horses are going faster than ever due to the progress of technology, gait purification, and other innovations, but one thing has never changed --- the passion and love the horsemen have for harness racing and their horses.

Much of the attention in the sport goes to the magnificent horses and drivers who guide them to victory. But just as important is the tireless work of the men and women behind the scenes, such as race secretaries, racetrack announcers, management and caretakers.

This section of the book is dedicated to the people who have put their blood, sweat, and tears into helping harness racing thrive and survive through the decades.

Also, the generations of family members ---- from great-grandparents to the young horsemen and horsewomen today who chose to follow their ancestors in sustaining harness racing's stature --- THIS ONE'S FOR YOU!

(Please note that we have tried to acknowledge as many as possible, but unfortunately, we only have so much space.)

CHAPTER ONE

"Race Secretaries, Race Announcers and Management"

"Roger Huston --- "The Voice"

RACE SECRETARIES

Race secretaries are very important, for they "keep the lights on." Their job is not easy; for they must make a racing program with full fields that remain as competitive as possible.

Below is a list of some of the race secretaries who throughout the years have fulfilled their duties to management, horsemen and horseplayers in keeping horse racing engaging, exciting and viable.

LIBERTY BELL PARK

JAMES M. LYNCH: In tracks all over the country, in positions ranging from steward, to race secretary, to director of racing to general manager, James Lynch was a powerful figure in the sport for over 40 years.

In his early years, Lynch did some amateur driving and worked as a groom. After serving in World War II following a brief period as a schoolteacher, Lynch turned to harness racing full-time. In 1947, he began his lifelong vocation as a steward at Bay State in Massachusetts before assuming the position of race secretary at tracks in Ohio, Maryland, Florida, Michigan and Delaware.

It was in Pennsylvania where he settled the longest, serving as director of the United States Trotting Association. Lynch closed out his career as a general manager at Foxboro Raceway. Every year, The James Lynch Memorial at Pocono honors his many contributions.

HOLLYWOOD CASINO AT THE MEADOWS

JOE DeFRANK: He was the first race secretary at The Meadows and remained there for two years. He was admired and liked by all, especially the horsemen. Although there was a horse shortage at the time he was race secretary, he found ways to assemble competitive fields, even if it meant asking trainers to race horses twice on the same card, which was not unheard of in the heat- racing era.

After serving as The Meadows race secretary, DeFrank served similar positions at Brandywine, Windsor, Northfield and the Meadowlands before retiring in 2001. He was inducted into the Harness Hall of Fame in 1993. He once said, *"I never applied for a job racing. The job always sought me."*

BILL CONNORS: Bill Connors was the second race secretary at The Meadows, replacing DeFrank.

KEN MARSHALL: In 2020-2021, Ken Marshall was inducted into the Harness Racing Living Hall of Fame. Good friend Tom Charters remembers Marshall: *When I was assistant race secretary to Ken, he taught me so much. He was one of the finest race secretaries in the sport He provided me with a lifelong respect for the rule book and emphasized to me that the race secretary's position was the most important job at the racetrack.*

TOM CHARTERS: Few people involved in harness racing can boast the resume and credentials of Tom Charters. At one time he was part of the training team for the great mare *Delmonica Hanover*, caring for her as a 2-year-old and later when she was 5. They traveled throughout Europe, where *Delmonica Hanover* set records and would go on to become "one of the great trotters in history."

From 1976 to 1979, Charters acted as assistant race secretary to Ken Marshall. When Marshall left to be race secretary at Pompano Park, Charters succeeded him at The Meadows and remained there until 1982.

After his time at The Meadows, he served as director of racing in Macao. Charters later served as president and CEO of the Hambletonian Society/Breeders Crown.

Charters, a lifelong friend of Delvin Miller, said, "*The Meadows and Meadow Lands Farm became my second home. In 1969, I wrote to Delvin asking for a job and thus began a lifelong mentorship and friendship that would last until his death.*

My most memorable Adios while I was the Race Secretary was in 1980. Disappointed that we couldn't get the connections of Niatross to agree among themselves to enter in The Adios, things quickly turned out for the better later in the week when Storm Damage won in 1:53.2--- shattering the world record."

CHARLIE BISHOP: Charlie Bishop came to The Meadows in 1983; prior to that he had worked at Liberty Bell. Before that, Bishop worked at Ocean Downs with Billy Perkins and Brandywine Racetrack with Ted Leonard.

He said the best aspects of working at The Meadows were the people: the management, horsemen, and his staff in the race office, especially his able-bodied Assistant Race Secretary Cricket Colbert.

After The Meadows, Bishop stayed in the Washington County area several years before moving back to Massachusetts.

GARY BUXTON: In 1981, Gary Buxton replaced Charters at The Meadows, becoming the sixth race secretary there.

Buxton recalls, *It was a pleasure to work with Delvin Miller, Joe Hardy and Ed Ryan. My time there brings back fond memories. I also enjoyed making friends with Terry Bove, Joe Hutchinson, and Curby Stillings.*

TOM LEASURE: Involved in harness racing his entire life, he started out as a groom and owner, hooking up with trainer/driver Ben Bolon.

He first became assistant race secretary under Charlie Bishop.

"The favorite part of my job is working with stake races – it's also the toughest job. You have the best horses, trainers, drivers and biggest owners in the business.

I have been very lucky to have been able to have a home, farm, and raised my children in one place—never having to leave The Meadows."

In 1985, Tom became race secretary at The Meadows and holds that position today. Along with his assistant Cricket Colbert, the two have gone through simulcasting, Call-a-Bet, OTBs and casinos.

THE DOWNS AT MOHEGAN SUN POCONO

TED LEONARD: Leonard has worked at every track in Illinois as a race official. During his career he also worked as race secretary at Pocono Downs, Northfield, Dover Downs, Pompano Park and Sportsman's Park.

RICK KANE: Kane is Pocono's present race secretary; it's the 17th racetrack at which he has worked. Kane's family was always involved in harness racing. When older brother Bobby, a driver/trainer, met with misfortune, younger brother Rick, who had just graduated from college, stepped in to help in the horse racing business.

Even Kane's mother worked in the program department at Pocono when Hurricane Agnes hit the area in 1972.

In 1977, Kane was hired as assistant race secretary Pocono and remains there today. His greatest accomplishment in the sport?

"I got rid of eliminations in main events and consolations. I started this at Chester and continue to do this here at Poconos in the Sunshine Stakes."

Kane has lived a colorful life as he once owned a bar in New England called "Cheers" and wrote and directed two original dramas while in college for the campus TV station.

HARRAH'S PHILADELPHIA CASINO & RACETRACK

RICK KANE: Yep, that guy again. Kane started out as assistant race secretary at Hinsdale Raceway in 1971. In 1987, he took over the position as race secretary at Brandywine Raceway.

In 1992, he was race secretary at Bangor Raceway and then went on to a similar position at the Topsham and Skowhegan fairs.

From 1995 to 1998, Kane was race secretary at Raceway Park and in 1999 – 2000, he served in that role at Ocean Downs before moving to Rockingham Park in 2005-2006. Harrah's Philadelphia was lucky to have Kane before he made Pocono his permanent home.

JOE AUGER: For five years Auger was assistant race secretary under Kane. Auger was appointed race secretary at Harrah's Philadelphia in 2011 and remains there today.

TRACK ANNOUNCERS

Calling a horse race is not an easy job. Think you can do it? Try it for one race and see how difficult it is! A race announcer must identify the positions of the horses during the race and point out any sudden moves. If a horse goes off stride or is involved in an accident, it is the track announcer's role to alert the other drivers.

The announcer has to memorize each horse and driver before a race to be able to quickly identify each entrant.

Announcers have their own unique ways of calling a race. Some are boisterous while others are more technical. Over the years, harness racing has had many great race announcers, one being the late Sam McKee. Without being too prejudiced, my favorite is and will always be "The Voice'" Roger Huston. With his crescendo cadence, Roger makes every race he calls, even a $3,000 claimer, sound like the Kentucky Derby.

In the United States, some of the best announcers were Mark Glickman, Ed Gorman, Jerry Glantz, Tom Durkin, Dave Johnson, Ken Middleton, Shannon "Sugar" Doyle, Frank Salive, Ken Warkentin, Gabe Prewitt, Roger Huston, Marty Adler, Robin Burns, Michael Chamberlain, Jack Lee, Carl Becker, and the well-known and highly respected Sam McKee, who passed away on March 17, 2017.

Although McKee is greatly missed by the sport and horsemen, I'm certain he is calling races at the Racetrack in the Sky. So with the utmost respect and love ---Sam McKee, this chapter is dedicated to you.

THE MEADOWS

CHARLIE HINKLE: Hinkle acted as track announcer from the track's opening in 1963 through 1967. He returned to The Meadows for two more seasons in 1974 and 1975.

Hinkle is famous for popularizing the phrase, *Here They All Come,"* which he would apply to stretch drives and, in basketball gigs, fast breaks.

KEN KADAR: He replaced Hinkle as race announcer at The Meadows from 1968 through 1973.

ROGER HUSTON: A native of Xenia, Ohio, Roger Huston was race announcer at The Meadows for over 40 years. Huston called his first race at The Meadows in 1976 and has been behind the microphone for more than 188,000 races.

Throughout his lengthy career, Huston has called races at The Red Mile, Pompano Park, Gator Downs, Seminole Turf Club, Calder Race Course and many county fairs in Ohio and Pennsylvania.

But that's not all, folks, for The Voice has been invited to call races at tracks in Canada, Australia, Sweden, Norway, Finland, Wales and Ireland.

The Keystone Chapter of the USHWA inducted Huston into its Hall of Fame in 2013. Today, he calls the races at many Ohio fairs and remains The Voice of the Little Brown Jug, one of the sport's most important and prestigious events.

Huston has made harness racing his entire life and even named his two daughters after racehorses: Cami Sue, after a horse that raced at The Red Mile, and Nevele, after Nevele's Pride.

JEFF ZIDEK: Beginning in 1987, Zidek acted as the backup announcer for Huston at The Meadows and many county fairs in Pennsylvania and Ohio. In 2019, he replaced Huston as full-time track announcer.

Besides calling races, Zidek has worked as publicist for the Pennsylvania Harness Racing Commission, serving the PA Fair circuit, and as a marketing consultant for the Meadows Standardbred Owners Association, as well as a track handicapper at The Meadows. In a credit that no other track announcer can claim, Zidek founded and headed the varsity bowling program at St. Vincent College.

POCONO

JIM BEVIGLIA: Beviglia has been calling races at Pocono for 15 years and has hosted the preview show for the last decade.

Beviglia often refers to the track at Pocono as *The Old Girl*. The reason? It's his way of personifying a five-eighths-mile oval made of dirt and his subtle way of saluting all those ghosts that somehow come alive again each night the starter calls the horses to the gate.

PA FAIR CIRCUIT

JIM McGETTIGAN: Nearly 50 years ago, a twenty-something man was playing in a band when his father took him aside and suggested that since he wasn't doing anything during the day, he should learn to take care of the horses they owned.

Today, at the age of 70, horseman Jim McGettigan is still enjoying a long career in harness racing as a trainer and an announcer on the PA Fair Circuit.

HARRAH'S PHILADELPHIA

SHANE BACON: For a short time, Bacon was the track announcer in 2006.

JAMES WITHERITE: From 2006 through 2010, Witherite was the track announcer. Besides race calling, Witherite occasionally performs as a bugler for major stakes events, and he is an accomplished jazz organist with several CDs to his credit. He also serves as assistant editor for *Hoof Beats*, the monthly magazine of the United States Trotting Association.

MICHAEL BOZICH: Bozich got started calling greyhound races in 1997 at the Birmingham Race Course in Alabama. From 2004-2013, he was track announcer at Hazel Park in Michigan.

He also acted as backup announcer at Parx and Pocono. Bozich has been the race announcer at Harrah's Philly since 2014 and is also part of the rotational broadcast team at The Meadowlands.

"Jeff Zidek"

MANAGEMENT

The people mentioned in this section are just as important as the drivers and trainers who may be better known. Without a strong management team, nothing will succeed. The Meadows had some of the hardest-working, loyal and dedicated personnel throughout the years. Sadly, some have been called back home to the Racetrack in the Sky. Although they may not be with us physically, they are "Gone But Never Forgotten."

(Much of the information in this section was taken from *The Meadows 50 Years Journal* written by members of USHWA.)

*****

BLACKHURST, POLLY & RANDY: Polly Blackhurst started working as a groom at The Meadows for Mickey Burke. In the '80s and '90s Polly served as parade marshal and today she drives the starting gate there as a regular part-timer. Her husband, Randy, served for many years as a judge at The Meadows, and he also served stints as a steward at two Thoroughbred tracks--- Mountaineer Park and Presque Isle Downs.

BUXTON, GARY: Known to his friends and fellow horsemen as "great, funny and entertaining," Buxton was a charter at the Carlisle Fair before working at Pocono. Later,, Buxton replaced Tom Charters at The Meadows as race secretary.

CHARTERS, TOM: Tom Charters has had one of the most colorful careers in harness racing. He started out as caretaker for one of the best mares in harness racing history, *Delmonica Hanover,* then served as assistant race secretary before succeeding Ken Marshall as The Meadows race secretary.

Together, The Meadows and Meadow Lands Farm were Charters' second home, as he recalls:. *Staying at the farm could be a celebrity adventure in itself --- from answering the phone when Perry Como happened to call on a Sunday afternoon, to an annual invitation to one of Delvin's famous Adios barn parties. The parade of celebrities, both at the farm and at the track, especially during Adios Week, was incredible with names as diverse as: Joe DiMaggio, Willie Mays, "Buffalo Bob" Smith, Jay "Tonto" Silverheels and Miss America Phyllis George.*

What made The Meadows so unique was Delvin Miller and his presence, his dynamic personality and his legacy.

My most memorable Adios while I was the racing secretary was in 1980. Disappointed that we couldn't get the connections of Niatross to agree among themselves to enter the Adios, things quickly turned out for the better when Storm Damage won in 1:53.2, shattering the world record.

COLBERT, MARIE "CRICKET": Colbert has been employed at The Meadows since 1984. She helps current race secretary Tom Leasure assemble top fields for stake races, among many other responsibilities.

Before signing on with the race office, Colbert ran a stable at The Meadows with her husband Howard. If you need accommodations when coming to town, or oversight of the production of trophies, you call Cricket. She does it all with a big smile on her face, and she's always ready, willing and able to help all.

COOK, RUBY: The late Ruby Cook worked at The Meadows for almost 50 years and was lucky enough to see four generations of horsemen and horsewomen grow old together.

She was the switchboard operator at The Meadows and "the voice" when people called in with questions, or wanting to speak to someone.

Ruby always had a sweet and inviting voice and never knew a stranger.

In the beginning all calls went through "her" switchboard when it was a "real switchboard."

She had been working for Bell Telephone when she drove a neighbor to The Meadows one day and applied for a job. *When they found out my background they hired me until they could hire someone permanently. That someone became me.*

Cook did it all: announcements, loose horses, accidents, calls for security, ambulances, "call your mother" reminders. She probably saw more action than all the judges, and she probably knew a lot of juicy racetrack gossip, too.

Cook was an avid Steeler fan and even traveled once to see Terry Bradshaw play in the Super Bowl.

After the passing of her dear friend and co-worker Quinton Patterson, she was heartbroken. Cook was the second person hired to work at The Meadows -- a month or more before it opened in the summer of 1963 and almost a year after Patterson's hiring.

DiDONATO, PASTOR JOE: Pastor Joe has served as track chaplain at The Meadows since 1993. Every Sunday, he performs a service for those who want to attend. If horsemen are injured, Pastor Joe visits them to cheer them up. He also runs The Annual Easter Egg Roll for horsemen's children and is a big part of The Meadows Charity Auction.

ERENSTEIN, JERRY: The late Jerry Erenstein was an attorney and fast-food magnate who served as Roger Huston's co-host on the *Meadows Racing Network.* Erenstein was passionate about harness racing and very knowledgeable.

GOLDBERG, NELSON: The late Nelson Goldberg was the founder of Total Communications Systems, which blazed a trail in mobile television units. He was the perfect match for The Meadows, which hired TCS to produce *The Meadows Racing Network.* TCS produced hundreds of sporting events, including many for Penn State.

GREENE, SANDIE: The late Sandie Greene worked at The Meadows in the '80s and became the first female race caller in harness racing by serving as Roger Huston's back-up.

HARDY, JOE: Born in 1923, Joe Hardy may be one of harness racing's oldest living legends. Hardy owned The Meadows, along with his close friend Ed Ryan, and was an important figure in the track's post Delvin years. Hardy also is the founder of

84 Lumber Company; he built Nemacolin Woodlands and at the age of 80 won an election as Fayette County commissioner.

JEANNOT, MIKE: At one time, the late Mike Jeannot was the president of Meadows Racing. In his years at the track, he operated The Meadows off-track sites in the 1990s, extended the reach of the account wagering system and the *MRN,* and was head of government relations, helping steer slots legislation through the PA General Assembly.

PATTERSON, QUINTON: He was a fixture at The Meadows the first person hired by racetrack founder Delvin Miller in 1961.

Patterson served as the track's grandstand maintenance manager for many years and was well liked by fans, horsemen and his fellow employees. Stan Bergstein once wrote a column about Quinton Patterson stating, *Quinton Patterson was a man that helped the "rich" as much as the "poor."*

An editorial appeared in the local paper after Patterson's death in 2006 that said, *Everyone can be replaced, but Quinton cannot be replaced in this world today.*

Patterson's good friend, Curby Welch Stillings, said, *To be ecclesiastically correct, St. Peter still holds the key to Heaven. Quinton just made him a duplicate.*

His friends and co-workers still smile when thinking of Patterson, calling him "the beating heart of the Meadows."

Each year during Adios Week, The Meadows honors his memory and contributions with the Quinton Patterson Adioo Volo, a Grand Circuit stake for 3-year-old filly pacers.

ROONEY, TOM: The Rooney name is one of the most well known names in the state of PA for its connections to sports, acting and politics, such as the majority owners and operators of the Pittsburgh Steelers. Their pedigree is royal -- starting with "The Chief," Art Rooney, longtime Steelers owner. It continues through Dan Rooney, who operated the Steelers and served as United States Ambassador to Ireland; Steelers owner Art Rooney II; Kate Mara, an actress and film producer, and Rooney Mara, an actress and rights activist. It also includes The Chief's nephew Tom Rooney, former marketing director for The Meadows. He says of his days at the track:

My memories of that time are some of the best in my life. I remember that era as "Barnum & Bailey at The Meadows." Ed Ryan was Barnum and Joe Hardy was Bailey. Ed and Joe were best friends from growing up together, and later, fierce competitors.

It was Ryan who got his schoolboy chum Hardy in the lumber business. At the time, Joe was laboring in the family jewelry business, Hardy & Hayes. Ryan needed a wholesale lumber supplier and thus, 84 Lumber was born.

The times of Ryan and Hardy in the horse racing business caught me in the middle of who could outdo the other. No idea was too crazy to entertain the racing fans and owners. Some of my favorite memories:

1. *We dressed the drivers in Halloween masks (in post parades) and came up with a "Trick or Treat Trifecta."*
2. *We brought the Dallas Cowboy Cheerleaders into town, and they did a routine on the track between races.*
3. *We had various celebrity races and even used ostriches for one.*
4. *We did live wrestling and boxing events.*
5. *We had the celebrity dog, Ashley Whippet, retrieve frisbees between races.*
6. *We brought in a psychic to predict races. (He couldn't pick his nose.)*
7. *We brought Herve Filion in to catch drive.*
8. *We had Pittsburgh Steelers kicker Matt Bahr kick field goals on the racetrack.*

Two other big events in my 1974-1980 tenure attributed to Ryan and Hardy were the recruitment of Roger Huston from Pompano Park and the introduction of Sunday racing.

RYAN, ED: When the late Ed Ryan and his partner Joe Hardy owned The Meadows in the immediate post-Delvin era, Ryan was a determined and visionary entrepreneur who was way ahead of the times. He was also the founder of Ryan Homes, which still ranks as one of the best homebuilders today. He created the *Meadows Racing Network* against the advice of seasoned cable TV executives who warned him it would be too costly.

Ryan was also an active philanthropist who, in 1992, organized relief for victims of Hurricane Andrew. As a horseman, Ed owned and drove such standouts as *Seven O'Clock* and *Knight Dandy*.

SUTTON, BOBBY & KATHLEEN: Ironically, Bobby was born on the farm owned by Delvin Miller for Sutton's father was the farm's primary caretaker and lived on the property.

Bob worked for Delvin Miller and lived on Meadowlands Farm, primarily breaking yearlings. Sutton became an employee at The Meadows when the track debuted as the first pari-mutuel horseracing track in western PA.

Sutton, now 82, remembers a man pulling up one day saying, *Hi son, I'm Delvin Miller and you're going to work for me now. About 15 years later, the harness track was about to open, and I got a job in the paddock area assisting horsemen. It led to a career as paddock judge and was the beginning of a marvelous personal experience that endured.*

Kathleen Sutton, Bob's wife, also played an important role in the administration of The Meadows, serving for many years as the clerk of course, responsible for the handling of all ownership papers.

WILLIAMS, STUART: Williams is an attorney who once co-owned The Meadows with Ed Ryan, Joe Hardy and Delvin Miller in the late 1980s. He's also a director of the Meadows Standardbred Owners Association. Along with his wife, Frani, the Williams' race horses under the *nom de course* Shanamphilaniklou ---an amalgamation of the names of the Williams children: Shane, Amanda, Philip, Elana, Niki and Louis.

WOHLMUTH, MARY: As manager and hostess of The Meadows 2:00 Club, the late Wohlmuth provided an intimate trackside spot for horse owners to dine, socialize and cheer on their horses. She founded the annual Meadows Auction for Charity, which has been a horsemen's holiday tradition for more than 20 years.

CHAPTER TWO

"People Behind The Scenes, Game Changers, Owners"

ALBATROSS: Listen to Ellen Harvey describing the early years of Albatross, who went on to become one of the sport's all-time great pacers: *As a youngster, Albatross had been a handful to deal with. I recall that my father, Harry Harvey, somehow acquired wrestling mats to line his stall with at Arden Downs because he kicked a lot. Dad also built a small paddock in the centerfield at the Arden County Fair for him, though I suppose other horses used it as well.*

I remember watching his first baby race from the Hill in front of the administration office, which he won in 2:07. People were stunned that it was such a fast race. I wouldn't say it was a cheer, but it was immediate buzz, people asking each other if they'd seen that saying, "wow, how fast."

We walked down to the paddock to see my dad after the races finished and folks were talking about it along the way."

Albatross won 59 of 71 starts and earned $1,201,477 and was an outstanding sire.

AZUR, FRAN: Azur has owned such standouts as *Hypnotic Blue Chip*, who won more than $1.53 million, but he's equally prominent for his philanthropy.

Beneficiaries include the Meadows Standardbred Owners Association and the Standardbred Retirement Foundation to which he donates a portion of his horses' earnings. Today, he operates a Beaver County horse ranch and, with his sons Bryan and Chris, founded Trigen Investments.

BARBERRY SPUR: Roy Davis' Barberry Spur was a champion, if there ever was one. Trained and sometimes driven by Hall of Famer Dick Stillings, the colt was a huge yearling that was extremely smart and athletic. His Adios win in 1986 was probably the most emotional of all for it was a hometown horse, driver/trainer and owner. He won the Adios final in 1:53.1; it was his fourth win in a row and seventh in 13 starts that year, including the Cane Pace at Yonkers.

BEEGLE, SAM; Sam Beegle has been a force in Pennsylvania racing for decades — on and off the track. Which is somewhat surprising, given that he grew up on a dairy farm and was more familiar with cows than horses. But when he showed cattle at the fairs, he also got to observe harness racing there and thought he might like it.

Then he married Kathy Heit whose father, George Heit, Jr., was a prominent Pennsylvania horseman. George immersed his son-in-law in the harness racing business, and Sam's career as a trainer, driver and breeder took off. In those early years, he regularly toured the PA fairs and also raced at Wheeling Downs. He's had fair champions as well as sires stake winners at the state's three pari-mutuel tracks.

He's still at it, racing horses with partner Carl Vizzi under the *nom de course* Ginger Tree. As a driver, he's approaching a career milestone. As the 2022 fairs season wound down, Beegle's career win total stood at 996.

His impact off the track may be even greater. Since 2010, Sam has served as president of the Pennsylvania Harness Horsemen's Association (PHHA), which represents horsemen and horsewomen at Pocono and Harrah's Philadelphia. He served a previous stint in that role as well.

As PHHA president, Sam has helped develop the rules, guidelines and practices that form the foundation for Keystone State harness racing in the simulcast/racino era.

Always outspoken, Sam once shared with the *Daily Racing Form* some of his conclusions based on decades in the business, to wit:

Best Horse Ever: Always B Miki.

Best Driver Ever: Mike Lachance.

Best Advice He Ever Got: Never piss off the presiding judge or racing secretary. That was the first thing my father-in-law taught me.

BENDIS, RANDY: For more than 30 years Bendis has trained horses at The Meadows, putting together a terrific career with more than 3,000 wins since 1991. He's assembled a revolving ownership group, including John and Janet Campbell, Susan and Frank Castelli, Reed Broadway, Tom Cope, Mike and Diane Novosel and Bill Varney.

Among his top performers was *Georgia Pacific,* a career winner of nearly $1.3 million who captured an elimination of the 2004 Adios before finishing second to *Timesarechanging* in the final.

BRUSCEMI, MIKE & MARK WEAVER: Mike Bruscemi, along with his partner, Mark Weaver, are the most active owners in the Ron Burke stable. Currently they own all or part of about 200 horses, including some of the best in the business.

CAMERON, NAN & PETE: At their farm a short distance from The Meadows, Nan Cameron and her late husband Wilfred "Pete" Cameron enjoyed success as breeders and owners. They bred and sold *Nan Cam*, dam of the world champion *Cam Fella,* one of harness racing's all-time greats. Racing under the name *Cam Land,* Nan Cameron and her daughter Wendy won the 2004 Breeders Crown Mare Pace with *Always Cam,* who had won the Jugette two years earlier. Pete Cameron operated Cameron Coca-Cola at its peak and was America's 10th largest bottler.

CAPONE, ALVIRA & BILL: Not only were Alvira and her late husband Bill successful Standardbred breeders and owners, but Bill was a force in the Meadows Standardbred Owners Association, chief financial officer of Koppers Co. and chairman of the Duquesne University Board of Trustees.

CASTELLI, SUSAN & FRANK: The Castellis are at the core of the ownership group that has teamed with trainer Randy Bendis for decades of success. Just as important, Frank worked behind the scenes to persuade the Pennsylvania Legislature to authorize casinos at racetracks in the state --- a major benefit for the Standardbred industry.

CHOQUETTE, AIMEE: A caretaker for Delvin Miller in 1963, the late Aimee Choquette supervised the stable's young stars as they toured the Grand Circuit. He was the caretaker of the champion mare *Delmonica Hanover* when she was victorious in the 1974 Prix d' Amerique.

DAVIS, ROY: Roy operated Royal Travel for years (located next to The Meadows), but when he began affixing the word "Spur" to his horses, he created a legacy. With top trainer Dick Stillings (who often drove), Team Spur won two Little Brown Jugs, a pair of Breeders Crowns, two Dan Patch awards, a Yonkers Trot, a Cane Pace and of course, the 1986 Adios with Barberry Spur.

FABIAN, DR. ANDREW J.: The late Andy Fabian was operating his dental practice in McMurray, PA when he attended a breeding seminar hosted by Delvin Miller. Intrigued by what he heard, he and his wife Linda set out to acquire a small band of broodmares. While they never had more than five broodmares at a time, they enjoyed uncommon success. For example, they bred McCluckey, dead-heat winner of the 1992 Yonkers Trot. In 2004, they sold Miss Wisconsin at the Kentucky Standardbred Sale. When future Hall of Famer Ron Gurfein signed the ticket for $150,000, she became the highest-priced trotting filly yearling at the sale.

GILLOCK, RICH: The current President of the Meadows Standardbred Owners Association, Rich Gillock has been a steady hand at the helm of the MSOA since he joined the board in 1994. A third-generation horseman, he's been a leading trainer at The Meadows for nearly three decades and is equally at home at a national stake race or the PA Fairs.

Ladbroke
Racing
The Meadows
NEW LIFE MARK, NEW TRACK RECORD & NATIONAL SEASONS RECORD
KENTUCKY BUCK
DRIVER-ROD BOLON
TRAINER-LOU GOANS
OWNER-JIM DAUMIT
SEPT 15, 1998
1:59:3
MR COAL PRD 2ND
SO FAR KOSM 3RD
1 MILE TROT
PURSE $2,600

"Lou Goans"

"Lou Goans with Kentucky Buck sets track record in 1998"

GOANS, LOU: Growing up in Meadville, PA., Lou had been working with riding horses when a friend recommended he apply for a job with the Boots Dunn stable. He did and worked for Boots for 11 years.

During the summer Boots would race at the fairs, and in the winter he would train on his farm. When asked about his boss, Goans said, *Boots was a hard worker. He instilled that in his help and expected us to take the best care of the horses. We started at 5 a.m., and most of the days we didn't finish until dinner time.*

In 1999, Goans left Dunn to go out on his own. His boss gave him a horse he could take with him and mess around with. At that time Lou also helped out trainer Rick Beinhauer.

When Adios Week came around, Goans would have to ship his stable from The Meadows because the stalls were needed for the stake horses coming in. Lou would take his horses to the Smithport Fairgrounds where he would sleep in the truck under a cooler blanket. He didn't get much sleep for there were numerous bears that wandered around the grounds at night.

His greatest fair memory: Lou once owned a 2-year-old, pacing-bred trotter named Kentucky Buck. (His sire was Kentucky Spur.) Lou took his horse to the fairs where he broke stride in every race. When he returned to The Meadows, he put Kentucky Buck in a race and not only did the horse win, but he also set a new track record of 1:59.2.

"Mark Goldberg"

GOLDBERG, MARK: Mark Goldberg grew up in Philadelphia and remembers going with his father, grandfather, and two brothers to Brandywine Raceway before Liberty Bell opened. He attended Temple University, bought a horse, left college and started grooming at Liberty Bell, working for trainers Bill Carroll and Bob Anderson. While there, Mark got to see Herve Filion dominate the driving colony in the United States.

In 1972, Mark moved to the Meadows and developed a stable. It took only a few years before he accumulated 15 to 20 horses and was the leading trainer in the late 70s & 80s. Goldberg used catch drivers, helping launch the careers of Neil Karp, Patsy Rapone, Dean Zaimes, Lewis Keith, Dave Palone and Tyler Stillings. Today, along with, Stillings, Mark operates a stable of horses racing mostly at The Meadows.

MAX HEMPT: The name Hempt is well known to anyone in harness racing, as all of the "Keystone" horses comes from Hempt Farms. He was an amateur driver, U.S.T.A. Director, and breeder. His Harrisburg area training center, *Hollyhurst*, served as the "test track" for the Tartan surface the winter before The Meadows opened.

HYLKEMA, HERMAN: The late Netherlands-born trainer Herman Hylkema is the one who started harness racing's "winningest" driver, Dave Palone, on his legendary career.

Hylkema was training for Dave's father, Butch Palone, when 15 year-old Dave asked if he could jog one of Hylkema's horses. He did, and the rest is history.

KEAN, ANDY: Kean is a second-generation horseman who inherited his love of horses from his dad. *My dad trained horses in the1960s and 1970s and ran a pretty big stable, racing the Brandywine and Liberty Bell circuit. I went to the Navy in 1968, and when I got out in 1972, I worked for a veterinarian for a year and claimed my first horse in the fall. I got out of the business in 1983 and took a job driving the starter gate alongside 'Shoe' (Norton Shoemaker) at Pocono. We've been working together ever since."*

(A portion of this story was written by Jennifer Starr for the Pennsylvania Horse Racing Association.)

KEY, BOB: A longtime breeder and owner and successful industrialist, the late Bob Key achieved national success with horses raised on his farm near Leechburg, PA. Perhaps the most notable is *American Winner,* who won the 1993 Hambletonian, then went on to a successful career as a stallion. Among his other top performers were *Break The Bank K,* who captured the 2010 Breeders Crown for 3-year-old colt trotters, *BJ's Pleasure,* a 2001 inductee of the Living Hall of Fame, and the siblings *Winning Mister* and *Win Missy B,* who each banked more than $1 million.

"Billy Mullen"

MULLEN, BILLY: Mullen started his racing career in 1972. Before going out on his own, he worked for Harry Harvey, Alan Meyer, and Dale Richards.

In 1978 trainer/driver Mullen went on his own and took his horses to Pocono to compete at the state-of-the-art racetrack.

Mullen says his favorite memories were meeting great people such as Steve Salerno and Greg Wasiluk.

Some of his best horses were *Fred's Hitter, Westland's Son* and *H.H. Claire.* Mullen loved racing his horses at Pocono, stating that he got spoiled and didn't like going anywhere else.

Asked why horses are going so much faster today, Mullen answered: *Definitely the breeding. Before, if you had a horse go a quarter in .27 seconds, you had a good one. Today they all do that. Today, we breed for speed.*

McMullen says the trainer he most admires is Jimmy Takter.

Today, Billy Mullen is 65 years old and still hard at it, training a small stable at Pocono ---the track he loves the most.

PIATT, JACK B. II: Although the Piatt family has owned horses at The Meadows for more than 35 years, they also owned and operated Meadow Lands Farm (Delvin Miller's home and the birthplace of Adios) from 1982 until 2002. A good friend and partner of trainer Dan Altmeyer, the two enjoyed many great horses during their collaboration --- such as Cambest, whose 1993 time trial mark of 1:46.1 at Springfield was at that time the fastest mile ever paced.

Currently, Jack serves as vice-president of the The Meadows Standardbred Owners Association Board of Directors.

PROSSER, LOU ANN: Lou Ann Prosser has lived a fairy tale life. She resided at Meadow Lands Farm for over 33 years and was lucky to be involved with the great sire *Adios*. She recalls:

Delvin Miller loved that horse so much. Adios had a double stall; a rail installed inside his stall to keep the horse safe from being cast; an air freshener so there was a pleasant aroma at all times, and even music piped in for Adios to chill to. When Adios died, Miller bought him a coffin made of stainless steel and welded his stall plaque on. He was buried in "his own field" and there were two beautiful trees planted to shade his champion's burial site.

ROSS, KENNY: A prominent automobile dealer (Kenny Ross Chevrolet), the late Kenny Ross may be best known for TV advertisements featuring the iconic "Aunt Penny." A devout Standardbred owner, Ross campaigned such top performers as *Tom Ridge.* Although Ross didn't drive in races regularly, he piloted *Crane Hanover* to a second-place finish in the 1969 Dexter Cup at Roosevelt Raceway.

SALERNO, STEVE: Steve Salerno started driving at Pocono in 1976 when he was a senior in high school. He was very successful right from the start and the leading driver at Pocono for several years in the '80s.

Knowing harness racing would be his life-long career, Steve bought a farm in New Jersey. For the next 10-to-15 years he raced his horses at The Meadowlands and Yonkers.

In the 1990s, Salerno relocated back to Pocono, where he remains today. Although Steve still trains a small stable, he hung up his driving colors, enlisting catch drivers for that job. Along with his wife, Emily, Salerno spends his days working on their farm.

SCHAMING, JIM: The late Jim Schaming was a devoted horse owner and board member of the Meadows Standardbred Owners Association. He also owned Mr. Magic Car Wash --- a South Hills institution. Whenever a racehorse surpassed $100,000 in earnings, the horse would be given a blanket in the winners' circle, sponsored by Schaming.

SHOEMAKER, NORTON ("Shoe"):
Known to everyone as "Shoe," he and his working partner Andy Kean have a combined 60-plus years of experience in harness racing. He says:

I was raised in the business. My father had racehorses and I worked for him. I started out racing at Liberty Bell and then began driving at Pocono Downs in 1975.

In the early 1980s, I had the track record with both a pacer and a trotter. The trotter, Buck Newton, belonged to Hanover Shoe Farms. I also raced in the Hambletonian one year.

Norton's driving career lasted for what he describes as "quite a while," but injuries eventually caught up with him.

Today, Shoe looks forward to the excitement of each and every race and working closely with starting gate driver Andy Kean.

(A portion of this story was written by Jennifer Starr for PHRA.)

"Pat Thomas"

THOMAS, PAT: When The Meadows opened in 1963, Pat Thomas of Eighty Four, PA took his stable of horses to race there. A fixture until the day he retired, Pat received the Outstanding Contributor's award for training.

In 1976 Thomas compiled a Universal Training Rating of .546, believed to be the highest ever at the track.

Over the years Thomas campaigned such fan favorites as *Berg Hanover* and *Roger Lobell.*

Following his death in 2020, The Meadows honored Pat Thomas with a Memorial Pace in 2021 during Adios season for his longtime achievements in the sport.

WASILUK, GREG: Wasiluk had a passion for harness racing at an early age: *My dad bought his first horse, a Standardbred, at Harrisburg when I was 5. We lived in New York City at the time, and I would go with him on the weekends and work in the barn. We moved to upstate New York soon after, and I would help him with the horses after school and on summer vacation. As I got older I did a work-study program with the horses.*

Wasiluk drove his first race at Goshen (Historic Race Track in New York) when he was 16, and at 17, he relocated to Pocono. There he worked for trainer Fred Heck, got his 'P' license, and the next year he went out on his own.

In 1982, Greg was tied with Bobby Williams for leading driver at Pocono, where he won a lot of sire stakes and Grand Circuit races. During his career Greg drove against some of the greatest drivers in harness racing, such as Bill O'Donnell and John Campbell, who were his idols.

Wasiluk was born with SVT (Supraventricular tachycardia)---electrical problems with his heart---so he made the decision to stop catch driving and just drove his own.

In 2008, Greg got his judge's license. He was a paddock judge and a starter at Yonkers, then a starter for three years at Vernon Downs, Tioga Downs, Monticello and Saratoga. A few years ago, Wasiluk hung up his trademark tie, left the Judge's booth and joined the Pennsylvania Harness Horsemen's Association as its representative at Pocono, monitoring the weather for race and qualifying days and checking the track conditions for safe driving for horses and horsemen.

(A portion of this story is credited to Jennifer Starr for PHRA.)

WILBURN, TOM: Known as a disciplinarian in the 1963 horsemen's colony, traine/ driver Tom Wilburn conducted religious services for his staff each Sunday morning. After his racing days, Wilburn became a successful cattle rancher and penned his autobiography.

CHAPTER THREE

"We Are Family: Harness Racing Families"

"Dan Altmeyer"

"Dan and Jeff Altmeyer"

In harness racing there are many families who eat, drink, and sleep the business. From great-grandparents to the young blood of today -- this chapter is dedicated to them.

As you read these stories, you'll notice the respect and camaraderie these horsemen have for one another. Racing at the fairs, as many of the families did and continue doing, was what they looked forward to every year.

Although it may be somewhat different today, for it's much more competitive, families still enjoy racing horses at the fairs and socializing with each other.

****

ALTMEYER, DAN, RUTH, TERRY, JEFF, JOEY, DAVE RANKIN, MIKE WILDER, HEATHER WILDER, SCARLETT WILDER & LAUREN WILDER: Sprouting from the Altmeyer family harness racing tree are many branches. Dan's wife, Ruth, was a Rankin --- a renowned name in harness racing. Ruth's brother, the late Dave Rankin, was a leading trainer/driver for decades in Pennsylvania and Ohio. Heather Wilder, daughter of Dan and Ruth and wife of top driver Mike Wilder, is a celebrity herself. She owns Standardbreds, hosts harness broadcasts and banquets and serves as president of USHWA's Keystone Chapter.

As a child, Dan had riding horses and initially found harness racing quite boring. When his father bought a harness horse, Dan became actively involved.

One day at the Dayton fairgrounds he met and was mentored by horseman Bernie Buzzard. It didn't take long before he fell in love with Standardbreds and horse racing. By asking questions and observing how it was done, Altmeyer quickly learned the ins and outs of the business and had a small stable for his new owners, Bill Kreutzer Sr. and Ken Leasure.

"I remember the time I told my grandmother I was going to race horses. She looked at me and asked, "But what are you going to do to make money!" laughs Dan.

As many horsemen, he loved racing at the fairs. The fair life was not only exciting, but it also was an annual family reunion.

"Every year we would close the house up in May and not return until the fairs were over. One day my friends and I went to Cadiz, Ohio, and a pretty girl caught my eye. That girl was Ruth Rankin, who would become my wife and mother of my two daughters."

Shortly later Bernie Buzzard decided to go to The Meadows and try his luck there, and Altmeyer followed.

"I met Bobby Sutton, the paddock judge, and we became great friends."

Sutton introduced him to Delvin Miller, who became a good friend and a great mentor who helped Dan a lot.

"Delvin was great. If I needed his advice on a horse, I made a call and he would come right over."

It didn't take long before some high-powered horse owners took notice of Altmeyer, such as John and Lucille Costello, Mel Blount (the former Pittsburgh Steeler) J.R. Ramsburg, and Jack Piatt II.

"One day Jack showed up at my barn and asked if I would train a horse for him. From that day on, we were partners and best friends."

Altmeyer went on a 20-year run that was second to none. His business plan was to race babies until after their 3-year-old year and then sell them. He would keep a percentage of the horses, which would eventually prove extremely profitable, for Dan owned many great champions over the years. The best was *Cambest,* who paced in 1:46.2 in 1993, at that time the fastest mile ever. Cambest went on to sire offspring that earned nearly $134.5 million.

Today, Altmeyer, although still involved in the business, has pretty much turned over his stable to his son-in-law Wilder. In the winter they train babies at Spring Garden Ranch in northern Florida and base at The Meadows in the summer. Dan and Ruth are the proud parents of two daughters and four grandchildren.

Two of those grandchildren are carrying on the tradition. Scarlett Wilder and Lauren Wilder, daughters of Heather and Mike, are active members of USHWA's Keystone Chapter.

"Terry Altmeyer"

The late Terry Altmeyer of Kittanning, PA, followed his brothers in harness racing, helping to keep it all in the family. Terry's love for horses, especially the "underdogs," was immeasurable. He loved taking a horse that had problems, doctoring him up, and making him a decent racehorse. Terry worked for his brother Dan before going on his own.

Although Terry competed in stake races, he absolutely loved racing at the fairs. He called it "cowboy" racing. During those days there was less hostility and rivalry between the drivers. It was more of a family rivalry, for everyone helped each other out.

Terry Altmeyer was known for wearing his "crocs." His daughter Megan's favorite memory was the time her father alongside his beloved family horse, *Tweedle Dum,* stood in the winner's circle, shirtless and wearing his crocs.

The Meadows honors him with the annual Terry Altmeyer Memorial Trot.

Jeff Altmeyer, Dan's cousin, aka/Uncle Jeff, loved rodeo events. In fact, he was a rodeo champion; but his true love was harness racing. One day he told his cousin Dan, *"I want to own a piece of every horse,"* so Dan founded Diamond Club Racing where Dan, Jeff, and Dan's son-in-law Mike Wilder all put in money and purchased several horses so that Jeff could watch the horses race every night.

Along with his family, Jeff owned and operated Altmeyers Trailer Sales & Western Wear --- one of the largest suppliers for horse people in the country and one of The Meadows' sponsors. After Jeff passed, his son Joey now runs the trailer business.

Rockingham Park..Nov.19,1973..Pace-One Mile....2:09

5 **NASSAU** — b g, 5, by Duane Hanover—Victory's Dream by Victory — Trainer-R. Battoni
Frank Joseph Gallo, Toms River, N.J. — PcD(⅝)2:09 1973 12 1 0 2 1,343
$00 — Driver-R. BATTONI, 8-26-49—BLUE-GOLD-WHITE — 1972 5 0 0 0

5

Black-Orange

11-12 Rock§	1100 ft nw1500 cd mi	31^2 $1:04^2$ 1:36 2:07	6	7	5	4°	$4^{7½}$	$5^{12½}$	$2:09^2$	2.40	(R.Battoni)	B.Dream,B.J.Dean,Tavern'sTime
10-31 Rock§	1200 ft 73nw3000 mi	30^3 $1:03^2$ 1:35 $2:05^4$	2	3	3	3	4^4	$3^{1¾}$	$2:06^1$	3.10	(R.Battoni)	DoctorSam,GreenacresD.,Nassau
10-20 Rock§	1300 ft 3500 clm cd mi	30^3 1:03 $1:34^4$ $2:07^2$	6	7	7	6	$5^{7¾}$	[illegible]	$2:07^3$	24.90	(R.Battoni)	LittleSpice,AdiosWillis,Nassau
10- 4 Rock	1200 ft 3000 clm cd mi	31^3 1:04 1:36 $2:08^1$	6	7	7	7	$7^{8¼}$	$4^{3½}$	$2:08^4$	57.00	(R.Battoni)	LittleSpice,G.Denton,Martina
9-15 PcD⅝	800 ft 2000 clm cd mi	30^3 $1:03^4$ $1:35^4$ 2:09	1	1	1	1	$1^{1½}$	$1^{¾}$	2:09	12.80	(R.Battoni)	Nassau,OllieTar,ByronDares
9- 7 PcD⅝	800 ft 2000 clm cd mi	31 1:04 1:36 2:09	6	7	7	7°	$7^{8½}$	$6^{6¼}$	$2:10^1$	19.80	(R.Battoni)	OllieTar,GreenR.Tiger,IrishAggie
8-31 PcD⅝	800 ft 1500 clm cd mi	32^1 $1:04^4$ 1:36 $2:07^4$	6	5	5	6	$6^{5½}$	$4^{7¾}$	$2:09^2$	21.90	(A.Lagreca)	JeremiahM.,Fr.E.Braden,PalmG.

"Ron Battoni"

BATTONI, RON & LINDA: Battoni got his start in the business in 1970 when he went to Ben White Racetrack and got a job working for trainers Tony Lagendo and Mike Gale.

Shortly after he got his driver's and trainer's licenses, he ventured out on his own, racing at Freehold Raceway, Foxboro and Rockingham Park.

During his driving days, he competed often with the "best of the best," namely John Campbell and Bill O'Donnell. Unfortunately, Battoni was involved in several serious racing accidents, which helped him make the decision to leave that end of the business.

His greatest memory was when he claimed *Peter Brooks* from Herve Filion. The first time Battoni raced *Peter Brooks,* Herve was in the race with another horse and parked Ron the entire mile, but Battoni still won!

Battoni was a generous man who would secretly buy horsemen dinners at times.

When he closed his stable, he joined the Pennsylvania Harness Horsemen's Association — eventually serving as PHHA executive director — and became patrol judge at Garden State. Ron's wife Linda has worked as the program director at Liberty Bell, Garden State, and Pocono Downs. In 2015 Battoni retired and enjoys the golden years.

(A portion of this story was written by Jennifer Starr for PHRA)

"The Earl Beal Family"

BEAL, EARL SR. & EARL, JR: This father and son team was always in the top training ranks. The older Beal was initially involved in auto racing and showed horses but eventually transferred to harness racing.

After selling their automobile dealership, father and son developed a stable of Standardbreds. But training wasn't enough for Earl, Jr., so he got his fair license in 1971 and pari-mutuel driving license in 1973.

In 1976, Earl, Jr. won 25 fair races and approximately 30 pari-mutuels. He received the leading driver award for Eastern Pennsylvania Fairs given by the PHHA. He also won the Bloomsburg Fair Stakes in 1976.

His greatest highlight was racing in the Hanover Stakes at Liberty Bell in 1976. Although he didn't win, Beal finished third to Hambletonian champion *Steve Lobell.*

A regular at Pocono, Beal raced at Liberty Bell, Brandywine, Yonkers and Roosevelt. He also competed at the Meadowlands, Freehold, Monticello, Buffalo, Ocean Downs and Dover Downs.

His favorite thing about the business was developing young horses.

Pocono hosts a rich stake every year called "The Earl Beal, Jr. Memorial Trot" for 3-year-old colts in memory of Earl Beal, Jr.

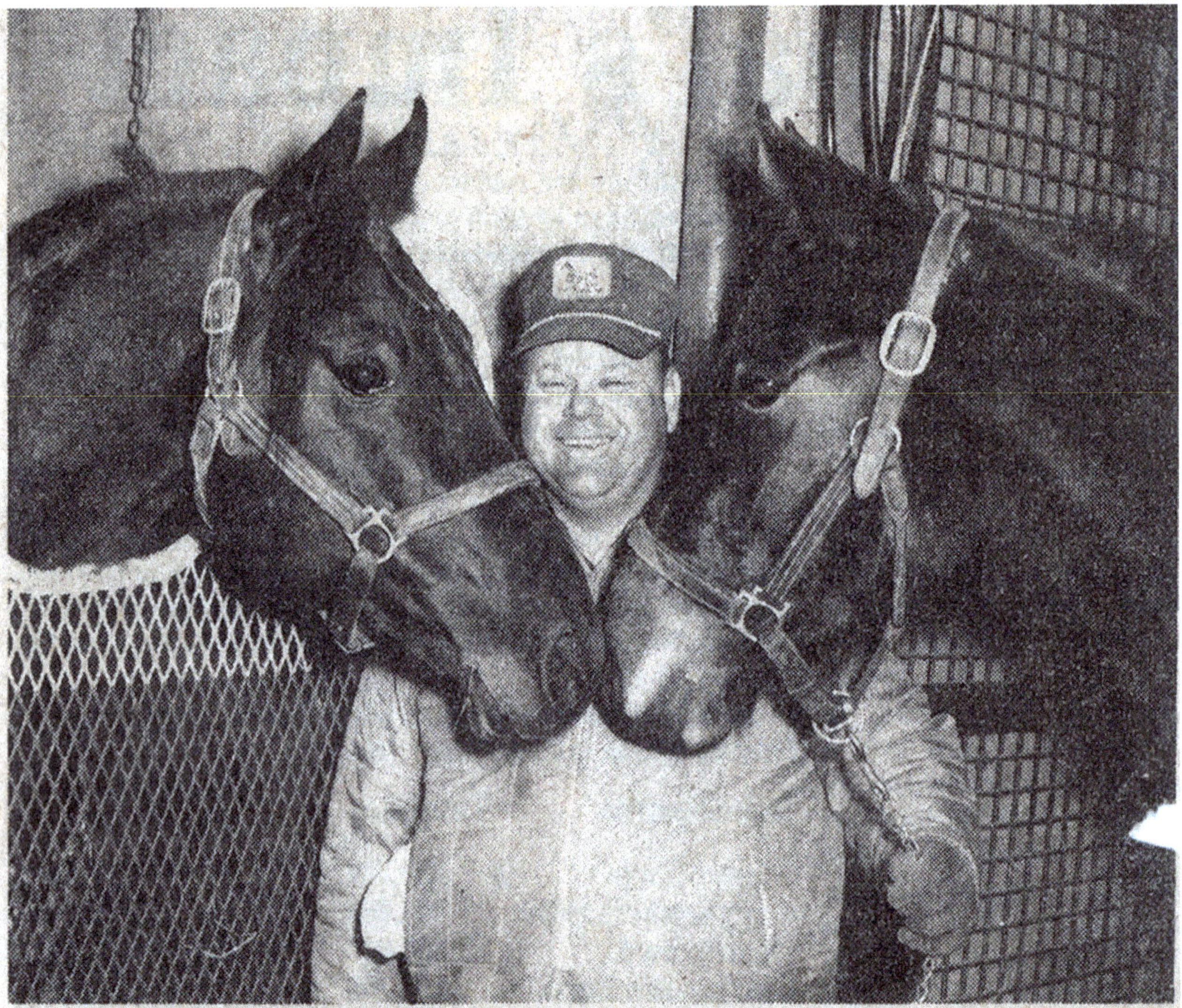

SON OF A BARON —George Beinhauer of Von Valley Farm, Scenery Hill, shows two reasons for a wide grin in this family portrait. At left is Von Baron, a popular invitational class pacer at The Meadows, and the winner of more than $143,000 in purse money. Tne eight-year-old pacer is the father of All Von, right, a two-year-old being prepared for his own career. Von Baron is scheduled for Friday night's feature as The Meadows opens a new 200-date harness schedule.

"George Beinhauer"

"The George Beinhauer Family"

BEINHAUER, FRITZ, GEORGE, ELLEN, LISA & AMANDA SHAW: Initially, Ferdinand Beinhauer operated a livery stable, along with a mortuary on the South Side of Pittsburgh. When he began racing horses under harness at Schenley Park, his youngest son, George, thought it was much more exciting than the mortuary business, so he went away to school to study animal husbandry. When he returned home, George along with his father and brothers Louis and Fritz founded Von Valley Farms and began racing horses at a new track in Washington County named The Meadows.

The reach of the Beinhauer brothers --- George and Fritz --- is long. George was one of The Meadows' bedrock trainer/drivers during the early years, producing such fan favorites as *Von Baron, Sweetheart Von* and many others. George was the trainer, and his daughter Lisa helped her dad in the barn and on the track, eventually training her own stable. George's wife Ellen was a judge at county fairs as well as The Meadows' paddock concessionaire. Today, Lisa serves as paddock judge while her daughter, Amanda, is a horse owner and trainer as well as a parade marshal at The Meadows.

Wait---there's more. Amanda is married to Jason Shaw, who operates a burgeoning stable at The Meadows. Jason's father Tom was a trainer while Tom's wife Carol is the current paddock concessionaire. Jason's brother is trainer/driver Chris Shaw and his wife, Ashley Brown is a trainer (and registered nurse). Ashley's brother is Brady Brown, one of the top young drivers at The Meadows.

You won't find many finer examples of harness racing's backbone of families.

(**Po**rtions of this story were written by Evan Pattak -- taken from *The Meadows--- 50 Years of Tradition,* and Pohla Smith, a *Pittsburgh Post-Gazette* sportswriter.)

"Rick Beinhauer and Sierra Kosmos"

BEINHAUER: RICK & REGINA: Rick Beinhauer is a third-generation horseman. As noted, his grandfather Ferdinand had a funeral business in the 1800s that provided carriages and horses. Before The Meadows opened, the Beinhauers raced at all the Ohio fairs.

Rick's favorite horse, *Mr. Simpson*, won 20 races in a row --- launching the Beinhauer legacy. Only 18-years-old when the Meadows opened, Rick worked in the stables for his dad Fritz and uncle George and notched his first career driving win during that inaugural meeting. Since then, he and his wife Regina have bred, owned and campaigned dozens of successful horses, most notably the world champion *Sierra Kosmos*, 3, 1:53.4 ($558,710).

Not only was *Sierra Kosmos* one of the best horses to come out of The Meadows, but he went on to become a leading stallion in the sport.

Today, Rick continues as an active trainer/driver at The Meadows; away from the track, he's a partner in Woodruff Family Services and the owner of Beinhauer Funeral Homes. Regina successfully breeds and raises cocker spaniels, winning many awards.

(A portion of the article was written by Evan Pattak, taken from *The Meadows---50 Years of Tradition.)*

"Betts wins a race"

BETTS, GIBBY & BARRY: Gibby Betts was a respected and well-liked horseman. When he started out in the business, he bought several horses for resale purposes but wound up keeping one. Throughout his career in harness racing, Gibby raced his stable all over the nation, including the Grand Circuit.

Among his many great horses was *Adios Killeen* ---a former Horse of the Year at the Meadows.

Gibby's son Barry started out following his dad by training and driving but quickly changed his mind and decided to become a veterinarian. Betts was a much-sought-after veterinarian, practicing mostly at The Meadows.

Dr. Betts met his wife Kim at the racetrack when she was working for trainer Bob Barker. Kim's father, John Shuba Jr., was also a trainer, and her Aunt Alice owned Keystone Harness & Tack in Lancaster, PA.

"Rod and Ben Bolon"

BOLON, PAUL, BEN, DARLA, RODNEY, SALLY & KYLE: The Bolon family originally came from Ohio -the Buckeye State. The late Paul Bolon, a well-known horseman, and his wife Irene produced five children. Oldest son Ben is now a retired Meadows trainer/driver, while son Rodney, an active trainer/driver, is married to the former Sally Parker, who works for the Burke Brigade. The merging of the Parker/Bolon families is why they are known as "The First Family of The Meadows."

Ben's wife Darla, also retired, was the winners' circle hostess at The Meadows while Rod and Sally's son, Kyle, is following his father, as he is also a trainer/driver at The Meadows.

Patriarch Paul and wife Irene have other grandchildren active in the sport. Greg Kahrig is a camera operator for *Meadows Live!*; his wife Kara owns horses while Spencer Kahrig, son of Kara and Greg, is a trainer/driver at The Meadows. Kent McGee, a grandson of Paul and Irene, is an Ohio-based horseman.

Many generations and lots of harness history are within this intertwined racing family.

(A portion of this story was written by Evan Pattak for Keystone USHWA.)

"Dave & Dean Brickell"

BRICKELL, THURMAN, DAVE, DEAN, SUE & MITCHELL YORK: Thurman Brickell owned a grocery store in Dayton, PA. The family always had riding horses, but one day Brickell decided to hire a horse trainer and purchased several Standardbreds. Along with his sons, Dave and Dean, Brickell would jog his horses at 4 a.m. before going to his real job at the grocery store.

The Brickells mainly raced at four fairs: Dayton, Indiana, Clearfield and Evansburg, for at that time racing was held at night, allowing Brickell to race after his day job. Remembers Dave:

The fairs were the best times. All the locals would get together and as we used to say, "What happens at the fairs stays at the fairs."

When they got older, Dave and Dean followed their father's passion and got into the business as Dave recalls:.

"Instead of working at the family store, my brother and I decided to get into harness racing. It was what we liked most and it kept us out of trouble. We would ship our horses to the fairs in a box truck and slept on a roll-up in the back of the truck."

Dean eventually became a schoolteacher, so when he was off in the summer, he would accompany the horses to the fairs in July and August while Dave worked for his uncle, Joe Hardy.

Also an important contributor from the Brickell family was the late Sue Brickell, Dean's wife. For many years, she served as clerk of course at the majority of PA fairs and also was a race secretary, a charter and a board member of the Pennsylvania Fair Harness Horsemen Association. She trained a generation of people how to serve in the various functions needed to keep the fairs going. She was a force, and her work supporting the fair horsemen and helping to make their financial situation secure earned her the 2008 Mary Lib Miller Award, the highest honor given by USHWA's Keystone Chapter.

Sue also was an accomplished horsewoman involved with several breeds. One of her favorite horses was the trotter *BS Woody,* who raced from age 2 to age 10. As a 3-year-old in 2005, *"Woody,"* whom Sue trained and co-owned with Dean, won his last 11 races on the fair circuit and then captured the Pennsylvania Fair Championship at Pocono.

Yet another noteworthy family member is Mitchell York, Dave Brickell's son-in-law. He served for 25 years as a Pennsylvania State Police officer before retiring and launching a second career as a Standardbred trainer. He's based in Cranberry, Butler County.

"The Brocious Family"

BROCIOUS, HAROLD, SARA, TOM LOUGHRY, JR. & ROBERT ROUGEAUX III: **P**atriarch Harold Brocious started his family in the business. When his brother-in-law bought a Standardbred, Harold bought in. That horse went on to win 14 races in a row. That's all it took for Brocious to be hooked and he eventually got into the breeding business buying several broodmares and standing stallions at his farm in Indiana County.

Harold also owned a coal business, which is where he got the excavation equipment to build a half-mile track on his 150-acre farm. Brocious and his wife had five daughters. Although they didn't follow their dad's passion for racing, their sons, Tom Loughry, Jr. and Robert Rougeaux III, did.

Brocious always encouraged his grandsons to "follow the process" by doing it the old way --- taking their time in developing the horses and doing their best. Says Loughry: *"The broodmares are our family members, and we try to keep the line going for our grandfather. He had a great eye for buying well-bred broodmares. That was his forte."*

Harold Brocious' legacy in horseracing continues today. Loughry and Rougeuax operate the stable and train the horses. (By the way, Rougeaux also is an in-demand equine dental technician who serves clients all over the East.) Sara Brocious—Harold's granddaughter --- is married to trainer/driver Kyle Bolon, and Kyle's mother, Sally, is the daughter of the late trainer Dwane Parker, a fixture at The Meadows for decades. A harness racing family tree for sure.

"The Brocklehurst Family"

BROCKLEHURST, PAUL, JOHN, HAROLD, MICHAEL & BRYCE: Harold knew as a youngster he wanted to make harness racing his career:

I couldn't wait until I graduated from school to get into the business. My grandfather Paul raced horses back in the 1950s, mostly at the fairs. He trained his horses at the Stoneboro Fair and was one of the "original" trainer/drivers at The Meadows when it first opened. He also raced at Buffalo, Batavia, Yonkers and Louisville during the winter.

My father, John, started his career in the '60s but had to wait until he got out of the service before going all in. Up until he got into a serious accident at Spring Garden Ranch back in the '90s, harness racing was his whole life.

Unable to continue training, he opened a shop at The Meadows repairing harnesses and equipment and did that for 25 years. He loved it and until his death five years ago, you could always find him in that trailer at the track.

Today, Harold's two sons –Michael and Bryce—train horses at The Meadows while Harold enjoys spending most of his time on his farm.

Harold's favorite thing about the business: *I love the challenge, especially training trotters and young horses. I have had claimers, but today my interest is in the youngsters.*

My wife, Rebecca and I train the babies and enjoy watching them become racehorses. Lately, I've been training a couple of fillies for my owners who prefer trotters. We have had a lot of success in buying the fillies at the sales, racing them and then breeding them. Their first foals are just now on the ground. Hopefully it's going to work out for them, but you need a lot of luck in this business. I also love racing at the PA fairs. I firmly believe that fair racing is the best education you can give a young horse. If they can go there, they can go anywhere for they get exposed to a lot.

"**Robert Brown with his horse, *Himself***"

BROWN, ROBERT, TERRY, BRADY & ASHLEY: Robert "Brownie" Brown was a police officer from Pittsburgh. After retiring from the force he started a career racing Standardbreds, stabling at the Butler County Fairgrounds.

After suffering a stroke, Brownie turned the reins over to his son, Terry, also a police officer. During their racing career, several of the Browns' top horses were *Himself, Oh Bob* and *Mary Belle.*

Continuing the family tradition are Robert's grandchildren, Brady Brown and Ashley Brown.

As small children, Ashley and Brady would do chores around the barn. It wasn't work to them, for they loved being around the horses.

Today, Ashley is a licensed nurse and trainer at The Meadows and is married to horseman Chris Shaw.

When Brady got older, he hooked up with trainer Steve Schoeffel, helping jog horses at the fairgrounds. Brady's first winning drive at The Meadows was in 2013 with *Luminosity.* Loving what he does, Brady now drives Schoeffel's entire stable.

He's become one of the tracks most active catch drivers, so adept at bringing home long shots that he's acquired the nickname "Downtown Brady Brown."

"A Young Florence Browne at Pocono Downs"

BROWNE, FRANK & FLORENCE: In the early summer of 1965, word was sent out that Pocono Downs would be opening for harness racing and horses were needed to fill the card.

At that time Frank Browne had a few cheap horses at Monticello, so he closed his house for the summer and moved to Pocono to race.

Browne soon became one of the regular catch drivers. In 1967, he trained *Frank A* --- his first good colt---- owned by Frank Arrico.

Frank stabled at Pocono Downs in 1965 and 1967. After that he raced mostly at Freehold, Liberty Bell, Yonkers, Roosevelt and the Meadowlands. He would ship the young ones to Pocono for education purposes then back to the New Jersey farm where he was stabled.

His favorite memory: In 1965, drivers still wore dark-colored work pants. When the ruling came out that drivers all had to wear white pants, the wives were in an uproar, concerned how they would scrub Pocono's famous red clay off their husbands' trousers.

Browne's daughter Florence, who often accompanied her father on his swings across the circuit, later became a harness driver.

"The Burke Family"

BURKE, MICKEY SR., SYLVIA, RON, MICKEY JR., BECKY, MELISSA & MICHELLE HILL: Mickey Burke Sr. paved the way for his family in the sport of harness racing. Little did he, or anyone else, realize that decades later, the Burkes would soar to the top of harness racing's training and earnings ranks..

When he was 18, Mickey Sr. was contracted by horseman Bert Corfield to train his jumping horses. At the time, Corfield owned several harness horses he raced at the fairs in PA and Ohio.

Corfield asked Mickey to come to the fairgrounds and sit behind a horse to which Mickey replied, *I don't want to ride that buggy—that's for old people.* But after jogging a horse, Mickey was hooked.

He went out and purchased a horse named *Hickory Buzz,* a two-horse single axle trailer, two jog carts and race bikes, equipment, and anything else they needed to get started in the business, for a whopping $600. That was in 1955. The next year Burke drove his first race at the Warren County Fair. Harness racing at that point was a hobby; Mickey owned a car dealership that kept him quite busy. It wasn't until he sold his business that he went "all in."

In 1964, Mickey married Sylvia, a union that produced five children. Not knowing how Dad could support his growing family, young Ronnie asked, *Dad, how are we gonna make a living?* When his dad answered, *We're gonna race horses, little* Ron replied, *Are you crazy?*

At that time Mickey had four $2,500-$3,000 claiming horses --- that was the start of an incomparable legacy.

Today, the Burke operation is a family affair. Patriarch Mickey, Sr. provides oversight and advice. Sylvia handles the financials with assistance from her daughter Becky while daughter Melissa Patterson owns Standardbreds. Ron assisted by brother Mickey, Jr., heads the training of six strings of horses that typically total 300 head or more. Michelle Hill, sister of Ron, Mickey, Jr., Becky and Melissa, manages the barn at The Meadows.

Ironically, when Ronnie was 12 or 13 years old, he was scared of horses. Well that certainly changed because today, Ron Burke is an icon in the sport. He's won more races — more than 13,000 and growing — and earned more in purses (north of $286 million) than any trainer in the history of harness racing.

Horses such as Sweet Lou, the fastest 2-year-old pacer of all time, and harness racing's richest horse, Foiled Again, who earned more than $7.6 million, are just two of the many champions that come from the Burke Brigade.

"The Meadows drivers"

"The Bush Family"

BUSH, HARRY & STEVE: Steve Bush is a second-generation horseman. His father, Harry, owned and trained Standardbreds but is probably better known for developing a leg lineament called "Harry's Leg Paint #6". Recalls Steve:

Dad was very good doctoring up horses with leg problems. He developed a leg paint and then sold the recipe. The leg paint has had much success; many horsemen swear by it.

My father believed you had to put a lot of time into your horse, and every horse's legs should be bandaged every day. The one thing 'really different' Dad did was to put 'staples' in the horses' ears. Every day my job was to spin the staple with a cow magnet. Dad said the spinning of the staple would send an impulse down the horse's leg to heal the problem -- and it really worked!

Steve worked for Hempt Farms before training for prominent owner Bob Key.

In 1992- 1993 I trained for Bob Key, developing a lot of stake horses and champions --- one being American Winner. In 1992 our stable earned $3 million in purses.

Harry is retired today, but his son Steve and daughter-in-law Kim keep the family legacy alive.

"Jim Chambers"

“Jim and Milford Chambers”

CHAMBERS, MITZI, JIM, CHRIS, MITZI & ANDREW NASER: Jim Chambers’ career in harness racing began when he was 15-years-old, working in The Meadows’ track kitchen as a short order cook. The next year his father bought into a horse with trainer Bucky Waugh, and Jim got his groom’s license. Jim worked with Bucky until the fall of 1970 when father and son started their own stable with a couple claimers. They raced the horses primarily at The Meadows and Wheeling Downs in West Virginia.

Chambers recalls,

With the advice of Delvin Miller and Bobby Sutton, Dad and I purchased our first yearling, Meadow Folly, from the Harrisburg sale. That Thorpe Hanover filly would become the foundation mare for my father and mother’s 47-acre farm -- Bustout Acres --- we started in 1975. The farm operated for 25 years, developing five world champions, some of which went on to race in seven different countries.

Dad remained active in the business for 31 years while still operating Chambers Insurance --- insuring many horsemen and stables at that time. My brother, Chris, began buying yearlings after graduating from college and raced them under the name C-Horse Stable. He had several stake winners, including Elway Hanover, who won the $50,000 Keystone Classic in 1992. Shortly after, Elway was sold to Swedish buyers.

Chris became president of Bustout Acres, served on the board of The Meadows Standardbred Owners Association and remained active for 20 years.

My sister, Mitzi Chambers (named for her father), began working at The Meadows in 1993 in the press box and also assisted with the Meadows Racing Network. She then moved on to the executive office and when the track was sold, Mitzi was head of Guest Services until March of 2020.

Mitzi's son, Andrew Naser, became the third generation to enter racing when he began working for his Uncle Jim in 2007 and remained there until Chambers retired in 2012. Andrew then worked for the Stillings/Goldberg stable, Ray and Kelly Paver, and on to the Norm Parker stable. Today, he's the go-to driver for trainer Kelly Stackowicz.

"Mark and Walter Christman"

"The Christman Family"

CHRISTMAN, WALTER, MARK, JOELENE & CHEYENNE: Mark and Joelene Christman are two of harness racing's greatest ambassadors. Mark's father, Walter, was a good friend of horseman John Townsend. They bought a few broodmares, starting Walter out in the business. Walter was also a die-hard fan who attended every Adios until he passed away.

Mark was attending high school at that time, but upon his graduation, father and son teamed up and purchased several racehorses.

Mark met his wife Joelene at the track; they immediately hit it off for they were "like minded" when it came to training horses. Joelene, also a barrel racer, trains her racehorses in an unconventional way. Instead of hooking nervous, "hot" horses to a sulky Joelene prefers exercising them under saddle.

Joelene is a third-generation horsewoman---her mother, Linda Armentrout, was a Meadows trainer for many years. As part of her multifaceted career, Joelene drives in amateur races and crafts racing-themed jewelry.

When Joelene met Mark they clicked and not only started dating, but they also formed a stable together. Their daughter, Cheyenne, is a horse lover who, along with her mother, is an advocate for rehabilitation and giving a horse who can no longer race a second career. She also works as an ambassador for the Ohio Harness Horsemen's Association.

“Mark, Joelene, and Cheyenne Christman with driver Brady Brown”

"The Corey Family"

COREY, BOB, SR., BOB, JR., JAY & PAUL: Bob Corey, Sr. from Canton, OH, was the patriarch who started his family in the sport they all loved: harness racing. In the beginning, Bob showed horses, but he soon got into harness racing and purchased several Standardbreds.

On opening night at The Meadows, Corey brought his horses to race at the new track in Washington, PA. He became friends with horsemen Delvin Miller, Gay Parker and Dick Brandt. Also an accomplished farrier, Bob shod many of Miller's trotters.

Eventually, Bob's sons, Jay, Bob, Jr. and Paul, all got involved in the business in some way. Jay was an owner. Bob, Jr. was originally a trainer and is now presiding judge at Running Aces, Paul, a trainer at The Meadows, recalls: *Dad would leave some horses at The Meadows with me while he raced at the fairs. Although I was in charge, he had trainer Bucky Waugh overlook matters and mentor me.*

We had a beautiful trotter named Skipper Gene Marx, who set a track record at The Meadows in 2:00.

When dad died in 2006, I went completely on my own and moved to The Meadows permanently in 2012. Harness racing has always been in our family. Sadly, I'm the last one to carry on our legacy.

The Meadows, PA

Sept. 18, 1982

BOBOS CONGA RHYTHM

William Daugherty, Jr., Owner
W. Daugherty, Jr., Trainer
Distance One Mile
Little Clay Boy 2nd

Wm. Fahy, Driver
Time 2:03.2
Purse $1,500
Christifer Mite 3rd

"Daughterty wins at The Meadows – 1982"

“Roger Huston and Dylan Daugherty”

DAUGHERTY, BILL, SR., BILL, JR., SUSAN, JIM, MICHELE, ROBERT & DYLAN: The Daugherty family's been in harness racing for generations and has the stories to prove it. Notes Bill, Jr.:

I have been in harness racing all my life. I can remember when the blacksmith would make horses' shoes by hand for $8.00 --- a far cry from what they cost today.

My father was a coal miner who would work around the horses in the summer when the mine shut down. Dad was known for buying a crippled horse, working to make him sound, and then taking him to the fairs.

When I was 16, I bought my first horse --- a 12-year-old Standardbred--- for $300. That's when I also got my driving license, and I couldn't wait to sit behind a horse in a race. Dad and I would ship from one fair to another. It was the best of times.

Back in the '60s the races were at night, and there was still a hub rail.

At that time, racing at the Erie fair, there were always two divisions.

It was always very, very foggy, making it hard to see. I remember one night when I was driving, the line broke in the stretch, and my horse took me on a nice scenic tour around the track in front of hundreds of fans --- we went a total of four laps and still finished second.

The family tradition continues today. Bill, Jr. trains a stable of 13 horses and owns most of them with his wife Susan., His sons, Jim and Robert, also train on their home track in Mercer, PA, while Jim and wife Michele own most of the horses in their stable. Dylan Daugherty, 12 year-old grandson of Susan and Bill, Jr, is well on his way to becoming a harness racing track announcer.

One day at the Waynesburg Fair, Roger Huston had to leave to catch a flight to Ireland and asked my grandson Dylan to finish calling the races for him. Not because he is my grandson, but Dylan called the last two races and did a wonderful job. He still helps call races in the summer at a couple fairs and loves it!

"The Red Douds Family"

DOUDS, RED, TOM BRICE, BART BRICE, & TODD BRICE: Red Douds was involved in harness racing his entire adult life. Racing mostly at the fairs Douds also competed at Buffalo and Batavia in western New York. When The Meadows opened, Red relocated to western PA.

Doud's daughter Priscilla married horseman Tom Brice --- a trainer who recalls the old days:

I remember when The Meadows opened and Bret Hanover was in the feature race. He was 1-9, and it had been raining all day. At that time there was the Tartan track and there were no harrows to remove the water, so they used a street sweeper. That night Stanley Dancer had Cardigan Bay and Su Mac Lac also in to race. When Su Mac was warming up, he freaked out when he saw the sweeper, caught a wheel over the hub rail, and ran until he collided with a post. Both the bike and horse flipped over."

Another thing I remember is at that time The Meadows had umbrella tables in the grandstand. One day John Simpson was training Ayres early in the morning. The horse got spooked, ejecting Simpson from the bike and kicked him in the head. Thankfully Simpson was not seriously hurt.

Those were the days when some of the greatest people were involved, such as Dick and Blaine Woods, Lou Rapone, Tony LaFace, Cecil Champion, Jim Schaming, Boots Dunn, Pete Cameron and the DeLallo family.

Tom's sons, Bart and Todd, often join him in ownership and breeding partnerships. Perhaps their best performer has been Miss Nittany, a success on the track and as a broodmare.

Says Bart:: *Those were the best times to be involved in harness racing. It was great growing up around the track, for the horsemen's kids were allowed in the paddock. There were times I sat between my grandfather and Billy Haughton or Delvin Miller.*

Adios Week was one big happy family reunion. The top trainers would ship in the horses for The Adios, along with overnight racehorses. Everyone would camp out, and it was a non-stop family affair. I am so glad we got to be involved in what was the best time in harness racing history.

"The Dunn Family"

DUNN, WILBUR, WALTER, DONNA, LESLIE, LISA & KATHY: The Dunn family has been in harness racing since the 1940s when patriarch Wilbur "Cubby" Dunn expanded his many enterprises into horse racing. As a teenager he had a team of horses for hire that he used to plow gardens and dig foundations. Cubby saved enough money to purchase a truck, which turned into multiple trucks. Eventually he opened W.L. Dunn Construction Co., but horses always held a special place in his heart. He passed that love of horses onto his sons, and they in turn passed it on to their children and grandchildren.

Cubby raced a stable of Standardbreds from the 1940s until his death in 1974. He operated Justadunn Farms, racing at fairs in both Ohio and Pennsylvania for decades.

Cubby eventually started a breeding operation that would supply most of his racehorses, all named with the "Justa" prefix. He employed several trainers who oversaw the everyday operations of his stable over the years. He guided mostly juvenile stock to much success and set many county fair track records in the 1970s. Some of the best were *Justalease, Justacinch* and *Justassuming*. *Justalease* still has direct offspring racing today, including the 2021 Ohio Sires Stake 3-year-old trotting champion and Grand Circuit stakes-placed filly *Herculisa.*

By the mid 1960s, Cubby's eldest son, Walter "Boots" Dunn, made the decision to concentrate on harness racing in addition to his full-time job running the family construction business. He started to take on almost all the driving responsibilities for Justadunn horses and began to purchase a few of his own horses, which were never given the "Justa" prefix.

Boots and his wife, Donna, typically campaigned a couple horses from the late 1960s until Cubby's death. Boots maintained his amateur driving status throughout his career and while driving mainly the family-owned horses, he was the UDRS champion for his category (100-299 starts) in 1973 and 1977.

It was in the 1980s when Boots and Donna started their own breeding operation. One of the foundation mares obtained from Del Miller was a prolific producer named *Armbro Delmonica*. Her top offspring, *Your Worst Nightmare*, was exported to Italy following successful campaigns as a 2- and 3-year-old at both the PA fairs and the pari-mutuel tracks.

During this decade, their daughters, Leslie and Lisa became more involved in the business, both as owners. Leslie also decided to get her trainer/driver's license. Her first driving win came at the Butler County Fair.

Another daughter, Kathy, started clerking at the Crawford County Fair and is still performing these duties at several PA fairs today.

During the '80s, Boots continued to add more wins and UDRS titles to his tally. By the end of the decade, he was closing in on 1,000 wins.

The '90s began with Boots earning his 1,000th win in April 1990. Although that win came at The Meadows, many of his victories were achieved on the PA fair circuit.

The mid '90s saw Leslie taking on more of the training duties until she relocated to The Meadows. Lisa eventually took over as trainer as well as manager of the breeding operation.

Boots started to cut back on his driving by the late '90s, although he did see limited action at the fairs. His last two starts were at his home track, Crawford County Fair, in 2011 and 2012. In true fashion, they were both winning drives. Boots finished his career with 1,152 driving wins, which is the most ever by an amateur driver.

Over the years, the Dunn family raced at every fair in the state. Cubby was one of the early board members of the Crawford County Fair while Boots was a board member for decades and was serving as its President at the time of his death.

Influential as the Dunn family has been, that reach is even greater today. Leslie is married to longtime Meadows standout trainer Bill Zendt while Kathy's husband is Leo Harvey, son of legendary trainer Harry Harvey.

“Boots Dunn Winning a Race”

"The Fahy Family"

FAHY, BOB, BILL & MOIRA: The year 1973 would be the start of a long and extremely successful career for young Bill Fahy. Relocating to The Meadows from New York with his father, Bob, Bill began getting catch drives after other trainers realized the talent Bill displayed.

My father and I brought a stable of horses to The Meadows to race, and I was lucky enough to get a lot of catch drives. I got my first start at the age of 14 racing in the New York matinees, and that's when I decided wanted to make harness racing my career.

I continued racing at The Meadows until 1984, winning the Adioo Volo with Turn The Tide and Naughty But Nice. That launched my career as a catch driver nationally.

I drove Jenna's Beach Boy and Western Hanover in major races, in addition to Florida Jewel in Europe. In 1998, I moved back to The Meadows with my wife, Moira (also a horse trainer who got her start at The Meadows in the 1980s) and our children Chelsea and Michael.

Our favorite all-time racehorse was Applecider Hanover, who with the help of trainer Norm Parker, won over $500,000. I continued racing at The Meadows until my wife and I retired in 2020. Today, we enjoy boating and camping."

"The Flickinger Family"

FLICKINGER, CHARLES, FRED & CHARLIE: There are four generations of Flickingers in harness racing, starting with patriarch Charles, a farmer who began racing at Painesville, OH. Always a horseman, when he was 70 years old, Charles got his driving license.

His son, Fred ("Flick") drove and trained horses, too. Flick's son, Charlie, also trains, as does Charlie's son Brian. Flick's wife helped out in the barn and was said to have been an excellent groom.

Charlie remembers when he drove and won for his dad with a horse named *Single Foot*.

"As a kid we would go to the fairs in our old truck. We went from fair to fair and never came home until the fair circuit ended. It was the greatest time. At night we would eat sweet corn and hot dogs and during the day watch the races. You never worried about your kids because we took care of each others."

Patriarch Charles originally bought stock in the Stoneboro Fair, which has passed down through generations.

The Flickinger's are one of the original families who came to The Meadows when it opened and continue to race there.

"Rich Gillock"

"The Gillock Family"

GILLOCK, MIKE, RALPH, KEITH, COONEY, & RICH: The Gillock family has been in harness racing since the 1950s. Granddad Mike trained his horses in Belle Vernon on a racetrack that was built in a field, over a rock-covered road.

In the 1950s Mike raced mostly at the fairs, but also at Wheeling Downs. During that time there were no horse trailers for shipping so horsemen would build and use box stalls.

Most farmers owned their own stallion for covering their mares. There was no going to a horse sale to purchase yearlings as it 's done today. And if your horse could go a mile in 2:20, you most likely would win the race. A far cry from today!

Mike had four sons: Mike (Richie's dad), Ralph (Doc), Keith (Cappy) and Cooney (Bird). All except Mike followed their father into harness racing. Ralph, Keith and Cooney all trained and drove.

On Opening Night at The Meadows, they shipped in and won a pari-mutuel race. Rich loved horses and wanted to hang around the barn whenever he could. His grandfather would buy Rich a pony to break but then would sell him. Then he would buy Richie another pony to do the same... and so on and so on. Rich remembers his grandfather telling him, *You can't fall in love with the horses.*

Rich is glad he was raised during those times; he calls them "the greatest." His favorite all-time horse is *Amorous Wil,* a $1,200 purchase who made $500,000. Today, the Gillocks own a farm in Belle Vernon.

"Roger and Clay Hammer with Max Hempt"

HAMMER, CLAY & ROGER: In the sport of harness racing the name Hammer is well known---especially at the PA fairs. Clay Hammer was one of the best driver/trainers at the fairs and known as "The King of the Fairs."

He was a self-taught horseman who started his career at the Bedford County Fair. His son Roger would tag along with his dad to watch the races and eat sweet corn and hot dogs.

Clay kept a stable of around 12 – 14 horses. Roger started at a very young age helping his father around the barn and in the bike, jogging.

When Roger was old enough to have his own stable, father and son went their separate ways. At that time they owned a farm together, so Roger bought his dad out and continued training there.

In 2005, Rogers *Vivid Photo* defied all odds to win the prestigious Hambletonian. The son of *S J's Photo* was the richest trotter of that year and set multiple records.

Another great horse for Hammer was pacer *Keystone Luther,* a Little Brown Jug heat winner in 1994 and lifetime earner of $608,967.

Today, Roger can still be found racing and winning at the fairs and pari-mutuel tracks. His daughter Misti is not actively involved in the sport, but his grandson is and helps him out. Roger also has mentored such up-and-coming horsemen as Brady Brown.

"The Harrison-Shields Family"

HARRISON-SHIELDS: Harrison-Shields Stables was created by George Shields and Jack Harrison. For about 100 years the Harrison-Shields Stable raced in western Pennsylvania. After emigrating from England, Robert Shields, his wife and their two daughters opened a livery stable in Pittsburgh's East End. George, the sixth of seven Shields children, embraced his father's interest in the sport and began driving the family horses when he was in his teens. Between races, George would sell peanuts in the grandstand to make extra money.

Eventually Jack Harrison, George's nephew, took the lines when he was 15;, thus the Harrison-Shields Stable was created.

Jack was an overnight success as a horseman racing the fair circuit. Several horses Jack drove were *Bessie Main Scott* and *Ellis Dean.* When Jack joined the military to fight in WWII, the stable was turned over to professional drivers Ward Stoum, Clark McCoy, Carl Larsen and Dick Snyder.

Some of the horses raced during those years were *Larry Hal, Projectile* and *Silver Melody. Projectile* and *Silver Melody* were good enough to be put on the cover of *The Harness Horse.*

In the 1950s Cecil Champion became the new trainer/driver for the stable. . Some of the better Harrison-Shields horses during those years were two-time season champion trotter Demon Rum, Rum Runner, Rum Coke, The Lodger, Stormy Dream, Sweet Sixteen, Keystone Mary Al and Haiti Hanover, *Keystone Mary Al,* by the way, was named for Jack's wife Mary Al Harrison, a key participant in the stable.

When The Meadows opened on June 28, 1963, the Harrisons moved from their suburban home to a farm in North Strabane, Washington County, so Jack could be close to the racetrack. He also moved Harrison-Shields Transportation Company to Washington, PA.

During the summer meet at The Meadows in 1964, the Harrisons' two daughters served as outriders.

Jack's daughter Patricia recalls, *It was during that summer I solidified my friendship with Curby Welch Stillings. Our group of friends at that time included young drivers Dick Stillings, Ben Bolon, Frank Glessner, Tom Kirwan, Doug and Dane Snyder, Chuck and Lew Williams and Jerry Ross Jr.*

Their legacy continues as Patricia is the author of *Summers Chance, Rebel's Choice* and *Stable Girl.*

BARBA

Indiana County Fair, Indiana, Pennsylvania August 27, 1985
Owner: Tunnel Hill Farm, Hyde Park, Pennsylvania Photo By Linscott Photography
Driver: Leo Harvey Trophy By: R. H. Fleming Buick and Pontiac
3 Yr. Old Pa. Sire Stakes Filly Pace 30.3 1:02.2 1:34.2 2:03.3

"Leo Harvey winning a stake race"

“The Harry Harvey Stable”

HARVEY, HARRY, LEO & ELLEN: Harry Harvey served on The Meadows original board of directors and managed Delvin Miller’s Meadow Lands farm before starting his own stable in 1966.

Harvey, along with five brothers, grew up on a dairy farm in New England.

Always having an interest in horses and harness racing, Harvey contacted top trainer/ driver Tom Berry asking for a job, but Berry at first didn’t respond. Finally one day Harvey received a telegram from Berry asking Harry to meet him in Florida that November.

Harry worked for Tom for years until Berry slowed down; Harry shifted to up- and-coming trainer/driver Delvin Miller.

The Hall of Famer enjoyed a career as a trainer, breeder and developer of young horses. He won the 1953 Hambletonian with *Helicopter* but is best known as the developer of *Albatross*, whom Harvey bought sight-unseen as a yearling.

Albatross was quite a handful and kicked a lot, so Harvey acquired wrestling mats to line his stall. *Albatross* won his first baby race in 2:07, but the original owner, Bert James, sold him the next year to Stanley Dancer interests. Said Harvey: *Losing him was my biggest disappointment, but the world went on just the same.*

In 1968, Harvey left and Miller started a stable of his own. He bought a farm in Arden, a few miles from The Meadows, where he stood several stallions such as *Majestic Hanover (*last son *of Adios) and Vicar Hanover* (by *Torpid).*

In 1976 when the Meadowlands opened, Harry sold his PA farm and bought one in New Jersey; now training for new owners, such as the Rooneys, from Yonkers.

Leo worked for his dad for several years in New Jersey before starting his own stable in PA. He married Kathy Dunn (Boots’ daughter) and continued the Harvey legacy training and driving horses before leaving racing for the trucking industry. His sister Ellen for years headed the Harness Racing Communications component of the U.S.T.A. and remains an advocate for rehabilitating and adopting Standardbreds.

(A portion of this article was written by Evan Pattak.)

"The Indof Family"

INDOF, JEFF, FRANK, BRIAN & JEREMY: When he was growing up in Belle Vernon, Jeff Indof had a neighbor who raced Standardbreds. Young Jeff mucked stalls for him and, once in high school, worked summers for the Zendts and Rich Gillock. He recalls:

My family members were all coal miners and steelworkers, but once I got into racing, I got the bug. It stuck with me.

Eventually, he formed and operated his own stable — not the easiest thing to do, as he worked full time for the Rostraver Township Road Department. Today, he's an equipment operator and road supervisor for the department while continuing to maintain a small stable. By the way, if you see Jeff at the track, try hailing him by his childhood nickname, "Sponge." You'll get his attention.

Jeff's brothers, Frank and Brian, followed him into the Standardbred business, Frank as an owner, Brian as a trainer/driver. Frank also serves as an executive for Arcelor Mittal in Monessen.

The Indof influence extends into a second generation, as Jeff's son Jeremy is a trainer/driver at The Meadows. Though still a young man, Jeremy broke into the Top 10 in the 2022 Meadows driver standings.

Jeremy contributes in yet another way. Each year, when the Meadows Standardbred Owners Association celebrates "Dr. Seuss Week" with an appearance at a local school, Jeremy volunteers his time to read to students.

"The Johnston Family"

JOHNSTON, GARY, AARON & SHAWN: In harness racing the Johnston name---Gary and his sons, Aaron and Shawn---is well known at the fairs. Gary was brought up in the sport, along with his sisters Debbie Schoeffel and Tracy Chropek. It was certainly a family affair. Gary also serves on the board of the Meadows Standardbred Owners Association.

Gary's father, Bing, had a decent-sized stable in the '90s. Aaron remembers helping his grandfather jog his horses, but at that time he wasn't a big fan. That would change when Aaron turned 12 or 13 and obtained his driver's license at the age of 18. Along with wife, Jen, they operate a stable of 8 to12 horses.

Gary and Aaron both agree that their favorite part of working in the industry is socializing with other horsemen and horsewomen. As Aaron puts it:

Most people in the business end up just like family, despite the fact that you want to beat them every time you're on the track.

For his part, Shawn has become an in-demand catch driver at The Meadows.

(A portion of this story came from PHRA.)

"Lew and Cherie Keith with Sharp Kosmos"

KEITH, LEW, CHERIE & TODD: Lew was born in Carlisle, PA. While in high school he worked for a local veterinarian and raced trotting ponies in Mechanicsburg, PA.

He arrived at The Meadows in 1972 with a modest stable, yet in 1976, he won his first Meadows driving championship and went on to collect over 1,900 wins.

Lew served as an officer and president of the Meadow Standardbred Owners Association and director of the United States Trotting Association.

Lew's wife, Cherie, was born and raised in West Mifflin, PA. She received a B.S. in Animal Science at Pennsylvania State University. Cherie began working as a groom at The Meadows during her college years and went on to become one of the few female trainer/drivers at The Meadows.

In 1982, Lew and Cherie married, and their combined forces placed them on The Meadows top trainer/drivers lists for many years.

They trained and drove for numerous wonderful owners, and their stable produced some terrific horses, including world record holder, *Sharp Kosmos.* The tough campaigner won 80 times in 2:00 or faster—ranking him 10th on harness racing's all-time list in that category.

In 1994, Lew retired from harness racing to pursue a second career as a homebuilder and land developer. In 2000, Cherie closed the stable and joined Lew. Now they split their time between Key Largo and Washington, PA. Lew is an avid aviator and boater while Cherie still rides and shows Quarterhorses.

Lew's brother Todd remains an active trainer at The Meadows with a small but successful stable.

"Jack Kiger"

"The Jack Kiger Family"

KIGER, JACK, JOHN BUTENSCHOEN, JACKIE BUTENSCHOEN & TYLER BUTENSCHOEN: Jack Kiger was the first of four generations in harness racing. Born in Waynesburg, PA. Jack got involved with harness racing after serving in the Army.

Kiger was a horseman, driver, trainer and self-employed farrier---he was one of The Meadows' original blacksmiths---who once worked for Delvin Miller and Bob McCarrell. Jack's daughter, Jackie, continues her fathers' legacy in the business today along with her husband, trainer John Butenschoen.

John is a third generation horseman, originally from Illinois. After graduating from high school, John went to Pompano Park in Florida and worked for Delvin Miller. In the summer of 1983, Delvin sent young John with horses to the fairs in the summer and back to Pompano Park in the winter.

Fellow horseman and friend Bobby Sutton told John about a pretty girl named Jackie, but her father, Jack Kiger, would make sure he kept his daughter away from the boys.

As fate would have it, John met Jackie and asked her to groom a horse for him at the Greene County Fair. She accepted, and they began dating. One day when John went to pick up Jackie at her house, her father had a shotgun sitting on the table and said, *"If you are living with my daughter, you are going to do something about it."*

They had the rehearsal dinner on Thursday because the Adios horse sale was that day and the Adios final was on Saturday, so they couldn't get married until Sunday. They honeymooned at the Washington County Fair.

Today, the Butenschoen family is stabled in the Pocono area, and their influence continues to the next generation as their son, Tyler, manages the stable with his dad.

KIRWAN, TOM & SHARON: Tom Kirwan got his start in the business as a "runaway." When he was a teenager, he ran away from home and went to The Meadows seeking employment. He'd never sat behind a horse, but Kirwan was hired by trainer George Beinhauer. He lived on George's farm and was mentored by him, quickly learning the trade.

George began letting Kirwan train his horses, and soon Tom was good enough to drive. It wasn't long before Tom became one of The Meadows' leading drivers.

Kirwan met his wife Sharon, who also worked at The Meadows in the paddock. One time Sharon fell in love with one of their horses and begged Tom not to put him in a claiming race. To make sure Tom didn't, Sharon signed the horse over to a friend and retired him where she could visit him.

After Kirwan quit driving, he stayed at The Meadows working various jobs, including stall superintendent. Tom passed away and is deeply missed by his fellow horsemen. Sharon still works at the track, driving the golf cart to escort horsemen to the winners' circle.

"The Clarence Martin Family"

MARTIN, CLARENCE, SR., MARY, CLARENCE, JR. & LISA: Clarence, Sr.was heavily involved in harness racing. In a family of five boys, all followed their father's footsteps at one time or another, but only Clarence, Jr. remained involved.

A trainer and starting judge, he's been around horses since childhood, working with his father,. who was the leading driver at Pocono in 1966.

The great pacer *Temujin* (*Race Time-Silk Stockings)* was one of their top horses in 1981. Recalls Clarence, Jr.:

I worked for Continental Farms and with Lee Broglio before going out on my own in 1986. My mom, Mary Martin, was also involved as she took care of the books and helped groom horses when needed.

Martin's favorite memory? When Max Hempt held fair races at his farm Holly Hurst. His favorite horse: *"I had Infectious Laugh, a really nice filly, who won all but one race as a 2-year-old and was undefeated at age 3."*

Presently, besides training horses, Clarence, Jr. is a starter at county fairs.

His wife Mary has this advice to harness racing families: "*Stick together! It's truly a blessing to live this life".*

*(*A portion of the story was written by Jennifer Starr for PHRA.)

"Bill McMillan"

McMILLAN, BILL & BOB: In 1972, Bill McMillan got his start in harness racing when a co-worker took him to the races one night. He recalls:

I didn't know a pacer from a trotter when my buddy got me interested. We eventually bought a mare named Lady Volovette, and I've had horses ever since.

McMillan, with owners Edward and Eleanor Clegg, started claiming horses, dividing time between Wheeling and The Meadows. Bill purchased a cheap claimer and taught himself to drive.

Training at the Butler County Fairgrounds, Bill would go to the barn after his night shift as a machinist was over .One of his best horses, *Flying Stone,* won every fair race and raced against *Fan Hanover.*

Bill's son Bob worked for trainers Linda Toscano, Bruce and Gene Riegle and the Burkes, but today works for the Altmeyer/Wilder Stable, splitting his time between The Meadows in the summer and Spring Garden Ranch in the winter.

"John McMullen"

MCMULLEN, JOHN & JUDY: When John McMullen was only 8, his father bought his first Standardbred. The family always had saddle horses, but after moving to Indiana, PA, the patriarch invested in his first racehorse.

A horseman from Indiana named Herman Nickle took McMullen under his wing and showed him the trade. John immediately fell in love with the sport, so he bought a farm and built a track. He raced mostly at the fairs, enjoying success there.

In his career, McMullen and wife Judy, from their base in Armagh, Indiana County, have campaigned several good horses. *All Set Let's Go* was one of them. When she raced at the fairs, announcer Roger Huston would say, *All Set Let's Go, and.... she's gone.*

The McMullens have paid unique homage to the Keystone State by naming many of their horses for Pennsylvania's 67 counties. They still have a few counties to cover.

"The John C. Miller Family"

MILLER, JOHN C., J. C., Jr., J.W., J.M., GARY & JORDAN: Now 93, patriarch John started the Miller family in the harness racing business.

He was raised on a farm when there were no tractors to do farm work -- only horses -- so young Miller began working with the horses when he was 12 years old---that was more than 80 years ago!

John showed Palominos, and one day at a show, Waynesburg veterinarian Dr. Marx told Miller, *You can't eat a blue ribbon. Why don't you get into harness racing and make some money.* So John did and purchased his first racehorse, *Gretchen Marx,* from the vet, whom he raced at Wheeling Downs.

One night after a race at Wheeling, Miller was called into the judges' office. Not knowing what he did wrong, Miller went in. Judge Briggs said, *If I had a movie of you, John, I'd make a mint.*

Back in those days, Miller did a lot of catch driving, and he went down with a horse in a race 10 times in 21 days.

Miller moved to The Meadows when it first opened, shuffling his stable between fairgrounds and The Meadows.

All four of Miller's sons — J.C. Jr,, J.W., J.M. and Gary---followed their father into racing as trainers or drivers. Grandson Jordan is keeping the legacy going, but you can still find Grandpa John fussing with the horses or growing and selling sweet corn he produces on his farm.

“The Napolitano Family”

NAPOLITANO, GEORGE, Jr. & ANTHONY: George Napolitano Jr. got into the horse business in an unusual way. When he asked his father why he got out of the business, his dad answered, *" Because he couldn't take the drivers. He swore that if he ever got back in the business, his sons would be driving."*

His father bought a few horses, and when George was in his early 30s (which is considered old for someone just starting to drive racehorses), he got his chance.

George is humble about his character-building years: he's become one of the leading drivers on the East Coast. In fact, George has won the dash title 15 times at Pocono, and he's bagged eight driving titles at Harrah's Philadelphia. In His career, he's amassed more than 11,000 wins and earnings exceeding $194 million.

Another Napolitano, younger brother Anthony, is also enjoying driving. He has been in the Top 3 in the driver standings at Pocono for several years and second to leading driver, big brother George.

As a kid, Anthony took care of his dad's stable and ran his stable at Pompano after their father passed away in 2006. He recalls: *I wasn't sure that harness racing was something I could do as a career. I had other things in mind, like be a professional boxer.*

He drove in the amateurs and soon got his 'A' license and made the transition to driving full-time professionally. After Anthony moved to PA, he bought a farm 20 minutes from Pocono, where he is based today.

Big brother George has nothing but praise and admiration for his little brother: *I put Anthony on his first win at Pocono. I told him "Ant, put this thing on the gate and roll him." And that's exactly what he did. He went in 1:51 and made the horse go faster than I did.*

One word that echoes from both Anthony and George is "thankful."

Both are thankful to be doing what they love every day, for their success, and for their strong family bond. I'm sure their father is looking down, smiling.

(A portion of this story is credited to Jennifer Starr for PHRA.)

"Terry O'Brien"

O'BRIEN, TERRY & CANDY: Terry O'Brien, a native of Canada, came to The Meadows before it even opened. Originally, he was the stable manager for his uncle, Hall of Fame trainer/driver Joe O'Brien.

While at The Meadows, Terry would visit the racing office regularly. One day, Race Secretary Joe DeFrank needed an assistant and asked if Terry would be interested. O'Brien said yes, as he recalls:

It was a good opportunity, so I arranged to take a couple months off from my uncle.

O'Brien, who was 23, at that time, became The Meadows assistant race secretary. He ended up doing that job with DeFrank at The Meadows and about four other tracks for a total of four summers. Terry also worked as a trainer for his uncle for four years.

I never liked clerical work and always wanted to be a trainer, O'Brien says. He spent the next six years training a small stable of his own during winters in Windsor, Ontario and summers at The Meadows.

In 1972, O'Brien moved to The Meadows permanently. Today, Terry is married to Candy O'Brien, also a trainer at The Meadows.

If you visit the O'Briens' Washington County homestead, you'll think you've wandered onto a latter-day Noah's Ark, as they rescue and care for all manner of animals.

"The Palone Family"

PALONE, BUTCH, DAVE, BETHANN & MIKE: At every harness track, there is one name with which most people identify. It might be Stanley Dancer at Yonkers, Bill Haughton ar Roosevelt.

When you hear The Meadows, that one person is Dave Palone. As of this writing, Dave has gone where no driver ever has and most likely will ever go again. On June 25, 2022, Palone collected career win 20,000---an unbelievable feat!

Standing in the winners' circle to congratulate Palone were his mother Jean; wife Bethann (herself a Standardbred owner; daughters Hannah, Alana, and Sophie, and grandson Asher. The only one missing was Dave's father, Butch, who I'm sure was looking down smiling.

Butch always loved horses and early on bought pleasure horses for the family to enjoy. He owned an automobile dealership which kept him quite busy, but when he could, he loved going to the racetrack with 10-year-old Dave tagging along. Dave immediately fell in love with the sport and told his dad, *"Someday I'm going to drive.*

One day Butch came home and told his wife Jean he was going to build a barn. At that time Jean was afraid of horses and said, *Just make sure you build the barn far away so we can't smell the odor.* Wanting to be more involved with her husband and son's passion, Jean began taking riding lessons; to her surprise, she loved it.

Butch bought a few broodmares, in addition to the racehorses he gave to trainer Herman Hylkema. Every day after school Dave would help Herman at the barn, and as soon as he could, he began driving in races. Although his parents wanted him to go to college, Dave's heart was in harness racing right from the start.

When Dave got hurt one time and was unable to care for their horses, his brother Mike, who was attending college, took a sabbatical and helped out. Mike was near graduating, but after working at the barn he also made harness racing his career. Today, he's a highly successful trainer at The Meadows.

If it weren't for Butch Palone's love for Standardbreds and harness racing, the sport might never have reached the milestone Dave Palone just passed and the history he has made.

"The Parker Family"

PARKER, DWANE, NORM, KATHY & REX: Calling him a successful and respected horse trainer only hints at the impact of horseman Dwane Parker. Dwane was a successful trainer whose horses earned more than $12.3 million.

In 1972, Dwane moved his family to PA from southeastern Ohio. He started out racing at Wheeling Downs then moved his stable to The Meadows thereafter.

Parker told his teenage son Norm to stay away from the barn, wanting him to make a smart decision about a career. But harness racing was in Norm's blood and after enrolling at Edinboro University and paying the deposit, the younger Parker knew that going to college would be fruitless.

Nairobi, was only one of many great ones that came from the Parker stable. After Dwane was injured, Norm took over the stable.

Besides Norm, the family tradition in harness racing continues through his sister Kathy, who was editor and general manager of *The Horseman & Fair World* and is now the editor of *Hoof Beats,* the monthly magazine of the USTA.

Kathy is married to Dan Coon, a noted racetrack designer. Another sibling, Sally, is a horse owner married to trainer/driver Rod Bolon, and their son Kyle is also a Meadows trainer/driver. Oh, and did we mention Dwane's late brother Rex, a longtime Standardbred owner?

It's all in the family.

The Parker clan displayed and celebrated their family each Adios Day with a bash known as "ParkerPalooza", where family and friends would gather on the Hill to enjoy the races---and each other's company. Sadly, Dwane passed away in late July 2022, but the spirit of Parker - Palooza lives on.

(A portion of this article was written by Evan Pattak for USHWA.)

"The Piatt Family"

PIATT, JACK, ROD, JACK II & JACK III: The Piatt name is one that is known and highly admired in harness racing. Their legacy began in 1968 through the friendships of Delvin Miller and Bob Beatty when Jack II and his father bought their first racehorse. Initially, Jack got involved, and then his brother Rod followed.

The Piatts were always active in the yearling market. Jack II's first trainer was Dick Hogan and his first horse was *Circle Thorpe.* He then hired trainer Ron Murin, and they enjoyed modest success.

Piatt then befriended trainer Dan Altmeyer and remained in business with him for 30-plus years. In fact, Altmeyer and Piatt had a 20-year run in the business that one can only dream of.

Piatt's father, a successful industrialist who founded Millcraft Industries, originally owned Meadow Lands Farm -- purchasing the land with the idea of developing homes. Due to undermining of the land, housing development was not possible.

It was at that time that Miller, who had the great *Arndon*, suggested since they could not build homes, they stand A*rndon* at Meadow Lands Farm. The Adios yearling sale was running at the time, in conjunction with Adios Week races, and the Piatts would sell approximately 40-50 horses at that sale. They also stood several stallions at Meadow Lands Farm besides *Arndon*, including *Mr. Dalrae.*

When the Piatts purchased Meadow Lands Farm from Miller, they retained Delvin's staff, who continued living and working the farm.

Brothers Rod and Jack eventually partnered and owned many great horses through the years. Jack and his wife Linnea had four sons---including Jack III (known as Jackie), who is involved heavily in the sport today.

"I loved breeding the horses and watching the babies grow and develop into racehorses. It was my happiest time---especially when we owned the great Cambest," Jack II said.

He has served on the board of the MSOA for the past 12 years while Rod served a stint on the Pennsylvania Harness Racing Commission.

"The Provost Family"

PROVOST, CHARLES, WATSON, WILLIAM, PATRICIA & BRAD: William Provost is the third generation of the Provost family. His grandfather Charles was the patriarch who started it all. Besides owning Provost Lumber Company, Charles owned Standardbreds. He started out racing at South Park then moved to The Meadows.

Charles and his wife Helen had three children---two boys and one girl---all of whom were involved in the sport. During the winter Charles would go to Florida to their winter home. One year his son Watson got to sit behind champion horse *Dale Frost,* sire of *Meadow Skipper,* trained by Jimmy Arthur---a memory he never forgot.

Charles was a good friend of Delvin Miller; at one time, they owned horses together. When The Meadows was under construction, the Provost family helped out through their lumber company. In fact, a lot of the boards used in the pole buildings at The Meadows were those from Provost Lumber Company.

Watson trained horses his entire life, and when he was ready to retire, his son William took over the stable. William is married to Jack Betts' daughter Carol. At one time Jack took care of superstars, *Im It, Ingenue* and *Steamin Demon.*

Watson's daughter, Patty, is a veterinarian at The Meadows. And the influence of the Provost family is continuing through a fourth generation, as Charles' great-grandson, Brad Provost, is a trainer/driver at The Meadows.

"The Rastetter Family"

RASTETTER, FRANK, RICHARD, JEAN & RON HARVEY: Originally, Richard started with Thoroughbreds but soon switched over to Standardbreds. It was in the early '70s when Richard and his brother Frank teamed up and got into the harness racing business. Richards' daughter Jean followed in her father's footsteps. Encouraged by her dad, she went all in.

Jean's most unforgettable memory in the sport is a horse they owned called *Exhibitionist,* who kicked her as she was walking by. Jean started driving in the '80s, winning her first race at the Crawford County fair, and held the track record there for a while.

She says that racing at the fairs was much easier in the earlier days than it is now.

Today, Jean is partnered with trainer Ron Harvey.

"The Ross Family"

"Memorial Race for Carol Ross"

ROSS, JERRY, SR, JERRY, JR., DAN, RON, CAROL & WENDY: Patriarch Jerry Ross Sr. was an Ohio native who began his racing career at The Meadows the day the gates opened. Jerry had three sons, Jerry, Jr. (Buster), Dan and Ron. All three trained and drove at The Meadows through the years.

Dan' s biggest moment was winning The Adios in 1997 with *Legacy of Power.* At that time the Rosses were only one of four local connections to win The Adios. *Legacy Of Power* remains the only horse to win The Adios through disqualification.

Throughout the 1980s and 1990s, the Ross family were regulars in the "Top 10" in driving and training statistics.

Jerry's daughter-in-law, Carol, was the outrider at The Meadows from the years 1982-1987. She brought beauty and class to the job for she rode her horse, *Smoke,* in an English saddle. Sadly, she passed away after a long battle with breast cancer. Her daughter, Wendy Ross, became an outrider at Tioga Downs and is now a leading harness racing commentator.

"The Salvi Family"

SALVI, JOHN & NICK: John Salvi grew up in Canonsburg, PA. When The Meadows opened, Salvi was drawn to the horses and quit his job to become a trainer. In just a few years, Salvi developed some of the better open-class horses of the early 1970s.

John's stable grew to become one of the leading barns in the 1980s with top performers *The Consigliori, Walking Boots, Ravenova* and *Damascus.*

Salvi's only child, Nick, is still heavily involved in the sport. Growing up on The Meadows' backstretch from age 12, Nick began working for his father early on.

When Nick was 18 he got his pari-mutuel license, so of course his father put him up. In 1977, Nick was the leading driver at The Meadows, and in 1978, he received the Peter Haughton Award.

Nick has worn many hats. He's been a racing secretary, a steward, a USTA director, a host on harness racing shows, and a starting gate driver., He's run the teletimer/ photo finish camera and at one time was an assistant for Hall of Fame trainer Ron Gurfein. Today, Nick is director of staking for Jeff Gural's racetracks.

"Tony Schadel"

SCHADEL, BRUCE, TANYA, TOOD, CHRISTINE, CODY, TONY & LINDA: The brothers Schadel, Todd and Tony, race separate stables, but they remain one tight harness racing family. Patriarch Bruce started it all, and wife Tanya served for many years as race secretary for the Gratz Fair. She's still involved with the fair board..

Their son Todd began working for trainer Don Wiest before going on his own, Todd learned a lot from Wiest—especially about trotters. *Lucky Mac Favorite* was Todd's first winner, launching his career. His favorite horse was *Peter Todd,* but *Vivid Photo*, winner of the 2005 Hambletonian, was his best. That one he co-owned with Roger Hammer. Today Todd is one of the PA fairs top drivers. His wife Christine owns many of the stable's horses with him while their son, Cody, is a trainer/driver who works regularly with the family's horses.,

Brother Tony worked for Todd before starting his own stable. Although it was small, when he married Linda, the number of horses increased. Linda comes from an Australian harness racing family. In fact, her sister is married to top driver Andrew McCarthy.

The Schadels have a very strong name at the PA fairs, as every year they win many races. They like to "stay close to their roots" and concentrate on making money, taking care of their horses and raising their family.

Tony and Linda own a farm--which just happens to connect with dad Bruce's land. Equipped with a treadmill, paddocks, exerciser and a 15-stall barn, they only have to go next door to train on Bruce's track.

Going to the fairs is something the entire family still enjoys.

"The Schadel Family"

SCHOEFFEL, TERRY, VIRGINIA, KATHY, STEVE, CHRIS & BROOKE: Steve Schoeffel is a name to be reckoned with on the fair circuit. Along with "The King of the Fairs" Roger Hammer, Steve has certainly had his share of wins through the years.

Terry and Virginia, Steve's parents, got into the business by '"luck,"---if you want to call it that. Says Virginia:

"One day my husband and I were taking a drive and passed Stoneboro Fair. I always loved horses, so we stopped to watch the races. Everyone was so friendly, and as we were talking, someone mentioned that if we wanted to get in the racing business, they knew someone who was selling out. That day we bought everything that man had, and that was our start in harness racing."

Whenever you saw Terry, he was carrying a race program. Harness racing became the Schoeffels' entire life, so it is no wonder Steve would follow. On June 28, 2022, Schoeffel set a new Butler County Fairgrounds track record with trotter *Big Baller Beane* winning in 2:02.1—a final clocking which knocked 3.2 seconds off the previous track standard set by *Toolbox.*

Kathy Schoeffel, Steve's wife, owns many of the stable's horses with Virginia while, Brooke, daughter of Kathy and Steve, is a caretaker for the stable. Yet another Schoeffel is involved — Chris, Steve's brother, a longtime blacksmith at The Meadows.

"The Dick Snyder Family"

SNYDER, DICK, DANE, CATHY, ALECIA, DANIELLE, DOUG, JAN & DOUGLAS: The Snyder legacy began with Dick's grandfather, who was a blacksmith. Dick Snyder was not only a great horseman, but, as a United States Coast Guardsman, he also was one of the only people who was "loaned" to both the Navy's special forces and the Army special forces in World War II. Dick was awarded the Silver Star for gallantry in action in the South Pacific and in 2018 the Coast Guard named and commissioned a cutter called *Richard Snyder* to commemorate his valorous service.

Eventually, Dick got into the horse racing business. In 1973, Dick and his sons Dane and Doug arrived at The Meadows with a small stable. His younger son Doug started catch driving and soon became one of the best at the track.

Through the years, The Snyders have campaigned some of The Meadows' top horses, such as *Keystone Savage, Rock Legend, Yankee Goddess, Barstow Hanover* and *Trusty Lobell.*

Dane recalls, "*When we first came here it was like one big happy family. Delvin made it comfortable for people to race at The Meadows.*

What was the secret to maintaining such a strong stable? *My father used to preach shoeing is the most important thing---especially with trotters.*

Dane and his wife Cathy---a longtime race charter at The Meadows---have two daughters, Alecia and Danielle, who are keeping their line going. Alecia cares for the horses while Danielle is a trainer and owner. Doug's wife Jan participates as an owner while their son, Douglas, has been a trainer/driver and now works for the Burke stable.

Today Dane goes training trips with Danielle like he used to do with his father.

I think about dad every day. I miss him a lot and wish I knew half as much as he knew," says Dane.

"Dick Stillings with friends"

STILLINGS, DICK & BUDDY: When you hear someone talking about a "Spur" horse, automatically you think of Dick Stillings. Dick, or "Dickie" as some call him, was and always will be one of the sport's best trainer/drivers.

A native of Mt. Vernon, Ohio, Stillings came to The Meadows in 1968 with a small stable of horses, venturing east in hope of finding success. And boy did he ever!

Roy Davis, a horse owner and founder of Royal Travel Agency, hired young Stillings, seeing something special in him---and the rest is history!

Dick said Roy was the best owner you could ever ask for. Every day Davis would come to the barn asking if there was anything his trainer needed. No complaints, no pressure, just an all-around perfect owner.

Together, Stillings and Davis built Team Spur, one of the most powerful harness racing stables in the nation. Their "barn team" consisted of Dick's brother, Charles "Buddy" Stillings, Christie MacIsaac and Cornell (Connie) Mallory.

Through the years Stillings developed great horses such as *Barberry Spur, Jaguar Spur, Kentucky Spur, Esquire Spur, Gunslinger Spur, Cheyenne Spur and Pegasus Spur,* among others.

Dick and his "Spurs" raced all across the nation---in the Yonkers Trot, North America Cup, Meadowlands Pace, Breeders Crown, The Graduate, The Adios, Little Brown Jug and Tattersalls Pace. But when the races were over, Dick always came back home to the Meadows.

One of his most memorable trips was to Hollywood Park in 1970-1971. When The Meadows meet ended in August, most horsemen would go to Wheeling Downs in West Virginia to race. One year John Salvi, a top trainer at The Meadows. asked Dick if he would go to Hollywood Park to drive his horses. At that time Salvi had a small but powerhouse stable of three horses: *Damascus, Walking Boots and Bengasi Hanover.* The team of Salvi and Stillings did very well at Hollywood Park, and Stillings did a lot of catch driving and was tied for leading driver.

Dick even wound up riding in the Rose Parade with the Rose Bowl queens. (I'm sure he didn't mind that too much.) But once again, when the meet ended, Stillings returned home to The Meadows.

Dick drove in a championship race in Russia and won the driving championship at Pompano Park one year.

Stillings will always remember the Adios races held at The Meadows. I personally remember one year when Dick won the Adios with Barberry Spur. Standing in the winners' circle was Mary Lou, Dick's wife, who worked the winners' circle during Adios Week, all dressed in purple---the color of The Adios. Stillings' "Uncle Lee" was a fixture, attending every Adios dressed in purple, wearing a tuxedo and top hat.

Dick Stillings was inducted in the Ohio Harness Hall of Fame in 2012; the Harness Horse Hall of Fame in Goshen, NY in 2013, and was awarded The Glen Garnsey "Trainer of The Year Award" by the Washington-Greene County Sports Hall of Fame. In 2022, Stillings was named The Little Brown Jug Wall of Fame Honoree.

Today, Dick is semi-retired. He owns a horse racing at The Meadows, and certain days you can find him at the MSOA office in the morning, drinking coffee. But one thing for sure---Dick Stillings always comes back home to The Meadows.

"The Stejcek Family"

STREJCEK, JOE & MIKE: Joe Stejcek worked in the steel mill. In 1969 under the guidance of trainer Chester Welch, Joe took a chance at harness racing. Immediately, he was enamored with the sport and Standarbreds.

Joe loved going from fair to fair with his horses, who were shipped back then in a homemade box stall. He was bitten by the bug and soon went into it on a bigger scale.

Strejcek bought a big RV and took his entire family with him on the road, closing up their house during the summer and racing mostly at the fairs. One of Joe's horses was a pony-sized filly named *Dressy Bessy he* purchased for $600 who turned out to be a decent racehorse.

Joe's son Mike followed his father and got a trainer/driver license when he was old enough. Mike says:

My dad was my biggest critic. He suggested I enroll at the Ohio Horse Shoeing School, so I learned the trade and added that to my resume. Dad passed away from Alzheimers, but horses and harness racing were with him until the day he died.

It was amazing that whenever we talked about racing or Dressy Bessy, Dad would snap out of it for a moment.

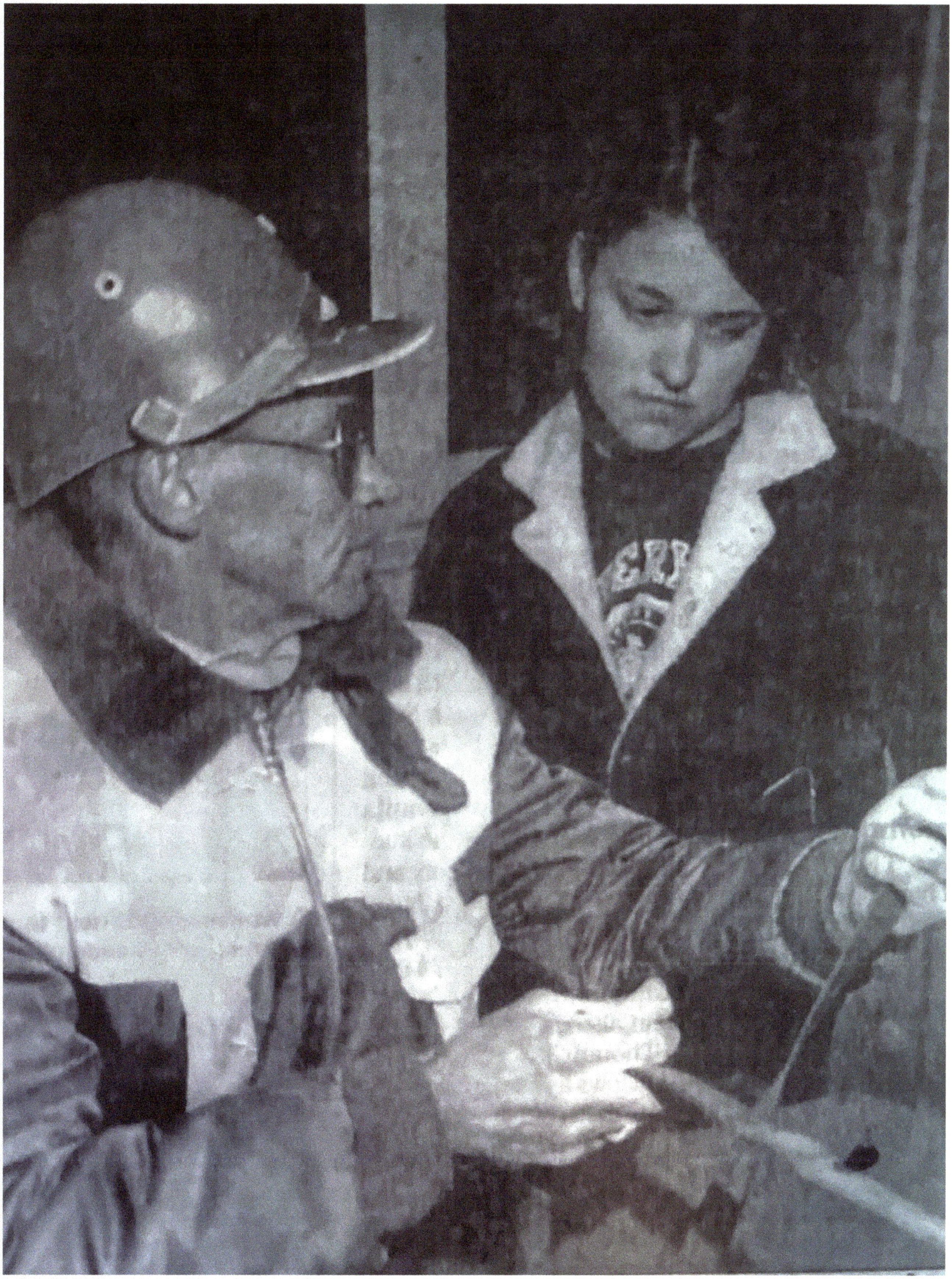

“Chester Welch and his daughter Curby”

"Tyler Stillings"

WELCH, CHESTER, CURBY STILLINGS & TYLER STILLINGS: When you talk about "coming full circle" in harness racing, one family that comes to mind is trainer/driver Chester Welch, daughter Curby Welch Stillings, and her son Tyler Stillings.

The family has been active in harness racing through four generations: Curby Welch (for whom his granddaughter was named), Curby's son Chester, Chester's daughter Curby, and her son, Tyler Stillings.

Chet (Chester) Welch got into harness racing in an unusual way: his father was an undertaker who had a livery stable in conjunction with his business, operating in the 800 block of 5th Avenue in Ford City, PA.

Chet was interested in horses as a young boy and got a lucky break when Roy Bowser, a neighbor and one-time famed harness racer, let Chet drive a sulky at the Clearfield County Fair in 1942. Welch soon became a name to be reckoned with driving at the fairs.

Chet owned and operated the Kittanning Tire and Recapping Service and drove in fair races as a hobby. In 1961, he decided to make harness racing a full-time career and began driving at Northfield Park in Ohio.

The "apple of his eye," daughter Curby, also fell in love with harness racing and began helping her father at the barn at an early age. Thus, began the Welch legacy. Although Welch had two sons, they did not have the passion their father had for horses and racing, as his only daughter did.

At that time women weren't allowed to drive in races, and most weren't allowed to work in the barn, but Curby set the pace. Back in those days, in a horse trainer's family, men outnumbered women 3-to-2, so the odds of the only daughter inheriting the trade were high. Today, it is much different, as many women not only follow their fathers' passion, but some outshine the older generation.

In 1971, Curby was quoted in a newspaper article saying," *I do believe there's a place on harness tracks for women drivers, and I do believe women could do their job once they obtained the necessary experience, but right now I have no inclination to seek a driver's license."*

Chester and Elfreda Welch's daughter certainly made a huge impact in the sport, as she's worn many different hats. When her father fell ill at 63, his daughter assumed the daily duties of conditioning horses.

For over 30 years Curby worked at The Meadows, and for the past 20 years, she has worked in the race office at The Red Mile. She also keeps the books and records for the Stillings/Goldberg stable of 40 horses at The Meadows.

Mark Goldberg, Curbys significant other for over 40 years, has been a leading trainer at The Meadows for decades, and her only son Tyler, now 50, is an accomplished trainer/driver following in his grandfather's footsteps. Notes Curby:

Tyler started working with Mark in the barn when he was 10 years old, and when he graduated from Duquesne University, he moved into the spot of trainer/driver for the stable.

Time flies when you're having fun. I have enjoyed the harness horse business for way over 50 years. I am 75 years young, and still at it. Racing has completely changed in the last 40 years for it is much more serious today, but I was lucky enough to be in it when it was work and fun. I'm still horsing around and happy to just be here."

The Welch family has come a full circle, indeed.

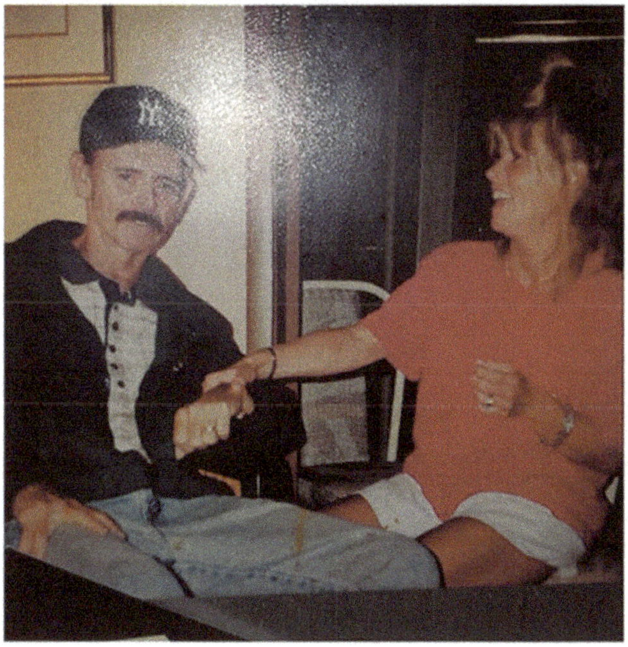

"Dennis Walsh"

WALSH, DENNIS & CHRIS: Chris Walsh's father Dennis was the first in the family to get into harness racing back in the '60s, as Chris recalls:

My father worked for Boeing and didn't like it, so when a friend of his in harness racing asked him to come help him jog horses, Dad fell in love.

He started working under a trainer (I believe it was Del Cameron) to learn the trade, and it wasn't long before Dad got his provisional driving license and then his qualifying license. He bought 6-to-10 Standardbreds and started racing them at Brandywine, Dover Downs and Roosevelt Raceway.

My dad met my mother Anna (Weezie) at the track for her family was also in the business.

Dennis got out of the business when his son Chris was born in 1992, but he missed it so bad that in 2008, he got back in, with son Chris working alongside him.

Dennis loved stabling and racing at Pocono, which he considers his home track. His favorite horse: *Radars Fella.*

His favorite memory in the business: *My father missed racing back in the days, for he said the camaraderie was so different. All the horsemen were friendly and rooted for one another.*

"Donna Weyant & Sandy Peterson"

WEYANT, DONNA & SANDY PETERSON: Georgiana Gunther and Leslie Marshall were Sandy Peterson's grandparents and the first to get into the sport. They were from Roaring Springs, PA and raced mostly at the Northern PA and New York tracks.

One day Peterson's friend, schoolteacher Donna Weyant took her to the races, along with another friend. They enjoyed it so much they decided to buy a racehorse and have been in it ever since.

Today, Weyant and Peterson are based in Bedford, PA.

“Wiest, Don, David and Justin”

WIEST, DON & DAVID: Over 65 years ago, a Standardbred trainer at the Gratz Fairgrounds approached an impressionable young 14-year-old he had seen hanging around and offered him a job helping with his stable. That boy was Don Wiest, who eventually made harness racing his life-long career.

“My family didn’t have a lot of money. I used to hang out at the fairgrounds and was offered a job pumping water for horses twice a day. That’s how I got started in the business.

In 1946 Roosevelt Raceway opened and I was invited to go to work. Since I didn’t like school. I quit and headed to Roosevelt. I was now making $50 a week taking care of five horses.”

Wiest drove his first race at Roosevelt Raceway, along with Stanley Dancer and Eddie Wheeler.

"We were three young kids getting into the business."

Don was drafted into the Korean War, and plans to work for leading driver Sanders Russell were put on hold. After being discharged, Russell met a pretty girl named Beverly.

"We got married thereafter and I got a job in PA as a tile setter but drove horses at the fairs. In 1965 I went full-time in the horse business, and within a week I had 20 horses."

Wiest also competed with harness racing greats Bill Mullin; Bill Popfinger; Joe Antonelli; Eddie Nickle and Jim Williard, He says the biggest change he's seen in the business in the last 50 to 60 years is "catch drivers."

"Years back older men were driving horses. Before that trainers generally drove their own horses. Today catch drivers jump right on them and go all they can because that's their living."

During his career Wiest collected 477 driving wins since 1977 when records were first recorded, and he was the trainer of 4-year-old trotter *Tui*, who won on a five-eighths in 1:52.3.

Today, the retired Wiest has turned over the operation of his stable to his son David, who also serves as president of the Gratz Fair Board.

"Wilbur Zendt"

SWANEE
Winner of the Second Race
Class C-2 Pace Purse $800.00
Oct.15,1960 Time 2:09
A New Record for Swanee
Trainer-Driver, W. Zendt
Owner, Glenn Shearer
Laurel Raceway Official Photo by
Alpert Productions

"Bill Zendt"

"The Zendt Family"

ZENDT, WILBUR, BILL, LESLIE, BRIAN, PHILLIP & BETHANN PALONE: Wilbur Zendt was one of the best "old time" trainers in the history of harness racing. Many people called him "the quiet man," but like E.F. Hutton, when he talked, people listened.

Originally a farmer of milk cows, Wilbur got his start in harness racing in 1949 when he went to the Port Royal Fair and saw Standardbred racing. It was love at first sight so he bought several horses and soon sold his cows, concentrating full time on the sport.

Wilbur's first win as a trainer was with *June Thumpus,* who just happened to win on the day Wilbur's only son Bill was born.

Wilbur raced at the fairs, but the purses weren't great, so he ventured to the big tracks, such as Steubenville, OH in 1950, then on to Painesville, Northfield, Grand View and Ocean Downs.

Originally, Wilbur trained at Bloomsburg, but in 1954 he built his own track and barn. He also shod his horses himself until the age of 85.

Wilbur's only son, Bill, started helping his dad at the barn when he was 9. He also helped build the track and barns, for Wilbur instilled in all three of his children the value of hard work.

After Bill graduated from college with a business degree, he focused full time on training Standardbreds and in 1970 started driving in races. In 1971, Bill drove at Northfield Park where his skills were quickly noticed. After three years working with his father, Bill decided to go on his own, so they split the stable 50/50.

In 1977, Bill moved to The Meadows and teamed up with Pete Cameron.

When splitting the stable up, Bill obtained four invitational pacers, which helped jumpstart Bill's career. *Natural Ability,* one of the four, was as tough as they come. *Natural Ability* raced until he was 14---the final year of eligibility for Standardbreds---and in his final year of racing won 19 of 30 starts. In 2002, Bill won the Jugette with Cameron's *Always Cam,* who came back to win the 2004 Breeders Crown Mare Pace.

Bill's two sons are both active at The Meadows, Phillip as a trainer, Brian as a trainer/driver. Daughter Bethann is married to Dave Palone while Bill's wife Leslie Dunn Zendt is a trainer and accomplished amateur driver.

EPILOGUE

It's been a long and winding road for chariot horses since those tumultuous days of Ben Hur back in the Roman Empire, not to forget all those stalwart steeds pulling war wagons so the masters could wage conflict on each other. We're quite a ways from that.

Nowadays, Standardbreds actually approach Thoroughbred clocking as those: 25 final quarters are almost commonplace at the mile track at the Meadowlands in New Jersey.

Closer to home: *The Palone Ranger* (Dave Palone) has just passed the 20,000 win mark at his home track at The Meadows---an incredible milestone which may never be surpassed.

Today we have three major racetracks in PA in addition to those all-important fair tracks. The horse industry is more than "holding its' own" as time marches on.

Certainly, the horses have never raced faster than they do now, and the demand for trotters and pacers is through the roof based on current sale prices.

The horse sales have never been better. The PA breeding industry remains at its apex through the auspices of Hanover Shoe Farms.

Whereas it has indeed been a long and winding road for our precious "chariot horses," it would appear things remain pretty much as is for the foreseeable future.

Personally, I don't see Palone's win record threatened in his lifetime. However, I wouldn't be surprised if a Standarbred paces the final quarter in :24 en route to a sub 1:45 mile. (Hello *Bulldog Hanover!)*

We've come a long way, baby!

TESTIMONIALS

I look back and think of the giants of our sport and who were domiciled in the Keystone State. If I were asked to pick the four (I cannot get it lower than that.) who had the greatest influence, I'd have Max Hempt, Lawrence Sheppard, Delvin Miller and John Simpson, Sr.

If it were only one, it would be Delvin Miller. He filled all the roles as a racetrack builder, breeder and a trainer/driver. He did it all, and he did it all well.

— Murray Brown,
director of Standardbred Horse Sales Company for 46-½ years

In the fall of 1968, I got a call from Harry Harvey and Delvin Miller. They wanted to know if I would come to western Pennsylvania and start an equine practice. That was my start at The Meadows and the great root of Standarbred history in Arden and Meadowlands, PA.

It gave me the opportunity to do breeding work along with racetrack practice. At that time The Meadows had only been open to racing for a few years, and shortly the licenses were expanded to 60 days each and later to 100 days each.

This made for a very busy schedule with foaling and breeding in the spring and racing in the summer, which eventually expanded to year round.

It was a rewarding time and God blessed me as I got to work on some great Adios mares and their offspring by world champion races horses. The great Delmonica Hanover was one of those mares.

That part of the country was a great place to live, and I was further blessed by the knowledge I gained from the excellent owners, trainers, grooms and farmhands as they passed on their love and passion of horses to me,

---- Wesley "Doc" Parry,
veterinarian at The Meadows from 1969 to 2005

SOURCES

The bulk of material used for this book is drawn from the archives of the United States Trotting Association, Wikipedia, Pennsylvania fairs and racetracks, as well as interviews with Keystone State horsemen, horsewomen and family members.

USHWA members, including Jennifer Starr and Evan Pattak, submitted certain information, photos and articles.

ABOUT THE AUTHOR

Born and raised in the Pittsburgh area, Howard trained horses at The Meadows in the late '70s and Pompano Park in the early '80s. With her husband, Pennsylvania auto magnate John Howard, she not only owned and campaigned super stars like *Efishnc* and *Neutrality* (trained by Bruce Nickells), but at one time was a guest commentator on *The Meadows Racing Network*, besides appearing in numerous commercials with her longtime friend, legend Roger Huston.

Later, in her second career as a published author, Victoria not only wrote *The Voice: The Story of Roger Huston,* but she also penned *The Kentucky Horse Park: Paradise Found* and *Gunner: An Enchanting Tale Of A Racehorse*---the inspiring story of a Standardbred rescued from obscurity who became a decorated police horse.

Victoria also co-wrote *Roosevelt Raceway: Where It All Began, Meadow Skipper: The Untold Story* and several children's books on Standardbred horses and horseracing.

Howard knows what she writes about, having lived through and personally been acquainted with many of the horses, horsemen, and families you'll be reading about in *Harness Racing in the Keystone State*.

Today, Howard lives in Florida with her dog, Max, and is the proud "Mom" to many racehorses.

INDEX

C

D

E

F

L

M

N

O

P

R

S

T

V

W

Y

Z

www.ingramcontent.com/pod-product-compliance
Lightning Source LLC
Jackson TN
JSHW071933020225
78184JS00013B/95
9781665573627